LEGAL PRACTICE HANDBOOK

LEGAL WRITING AND DRAFTING

To my father

LEGAL PRACTICE HANDBOOK

LEGAL WRITING AND DRAFTING

Paul Rylance

Series Editor: Anthony G. King, MA, Solicitor
Director of Education, Clifford Chance

OXFORD
UNIVERSITY PRESS

OXFORD

UNIVERSITY PRESS

Great Clarendon Street, Oxford OX2 6DP

Oxford University Press is a department of the University of Oxford.
It furthers the University's objective of excellence in research, scholarship,
and education by publishing worldwide in

Oxford New York

Auckland Bangkok Buenos Aires Cape Town Chennai
Dar es Salaam Delhi Hong Kong Istanbul Karachi Kolkata
Kuala Lumpur Madrid Melbourne Mexico City Mumbai Nairobi
São Paulo Shanghai Taipei Tokyo Toronto

Oxford is a registered trade mark of Oxford University Press
in the UK and in certain other countries

Published in the United States
by Oxford University Press Inc., New York

A Blackstone Press Book

© P Rylance 1994

British Library Cataloguing in Publications Data

A record for this book is available from the British Library

Library of Congress Cataloguing in Publications Data

Data applied for

ISBN 978-1-85431-169-6

11 12 13 14 15 16 17 18 19 20

Typeset by Style Photosetting Limited, Mayfield, East Sussex
Printed in Great Britain
on acid-free paper by
the MPG Books Group

Contents

2   Letters, Memoranda and Reports   66

3   Drafting   97

Preface

The ideas contained in this book are largely a result of the training programmes I have directed for a variety of firms of solicitors and the many helpful discussions I have had with practitioners, training professionals and other colleagues over the past seven years or so.

I am grateful for the help I have received from friends and colleagues, in particular, Tim Percival, Harnock Shoker, Diane Fasan, Karen Peacock, John Riley and Shama Kaistha. I would like to offer special thanks to Lesley Smith for typing the first draft and to Gillian Gates for her help throughout this project. I must also thank Tony King, the series editor, and Alistair MacQueen and Heather Saward of Blackstone Press for their enduring patience and support. Needless but customary to say, any faults are mine alone.

Introduction

'Be short, be simple, be human.'
(Sir Ernest Gowers, *'The Complete Plain Words'*, *third edition, 1986*)

'(1)   Never use a metaphor, simile, or other figure of speech which you are used to seeing in print.

(2)   Never use a long word when a short one will do.

(3)   If it is possible to cut a word out, always cut it out.

(4)   Never use the passive where you can use the active.

(5)   Never use a foreign phrase, a scientific word or a jargon word if you can think of an everyday English equivalent.

(6)   Break any of these rules sooner than say anything outright barbarous.'

(George Orwell, 'Politics and the English language', in *Collected Essays, Journalism and Letters of George Orwell*, vol. 4, ed. S. Orwell and I. Angus (London: Secker & Warburg, 1968)

'Lawyers have two common failings. One is that they do not write well and the other is that they think they do.'
(Carl Felsenfeld, 'The Plain English Movement in the United States' *Canadian Business Law Journal*, vol. 6, 1981–82)

AIMS

Although the art of legal writing and drafting has been practised for as long as there have been laws and lawyers, in this country at least, it is only recently that the subject has been recognised as worthy of serious study. Although many persist in thinking otherwise, lawyers have a poor reputation as writers. We are often accused of producing unintelligible documents, contracts and letters. It need not be this way. Modern legal language need not be, as Coode put it in 1843, 'intricate and barbarous'. People read legal writing, not because they want to, but because they have to. Lawyers need to learn to write in good, clear English that their clients understand. Those just starting out on a legal career should be given guidance in good practice from the outset so that bad habits are eliminated rather than perpetuated.

However, although I support the cause and I have attempted to incorporate plain English principles throughout, it is not the main aim of this text to mount a crusade on behalf of The National Consumer Council, The Plain English Campaign, Clarity for Lawyers or others who promote the use of plain English in legal writing. Although Chapter One addresses briefly the issue of correct grammar, this book is not primarily concerned with the rules of English grammar. Nor is this book intended as a reference text on English usage, even if it does attempt to highlight some of the more frequent misuses in legal writing. It is not a style guide but it does provide style guidelines. It does not purport or attempt to be a technical book on legal drafting although it does draw the reader's attention to some key technical issues. The book does contain many examples drawn from real documents but it is certainly not a precedent book.

In all these areas there are authoritative works of reference such as *The Complete Plain Words* by Sir Ernest Gowers and Fowler's *Modern English Usage*, and I have listed the titles in a bibliography at the end of the book. But, to date, no book has combined the main principles, rules and conventions in one volume for the benefit of newcomers to legal writing and drafting. In this book I have attempted to provide a basic but comprehensive guide — from the first stage of preparation to the final edit — for those just starting out on a legal career. Although the contents may be of interest to experienced practitioners, particularly where a firm is considering the establishment of a house-style, the book is directed mainly towards students studying the legal practice course, trainee solicitors and solicitors in the early stages of their careers in practice.

CHOICE OF TITLE AND LAYOUT

Tony King, the series editor, chose the title 'Effective Communication' for his book on lawyers' oral communication skills. This book might have claimed the same title since it is primarily concerned with effective communication, albeit written. I have settled for the functional 'Legal Writing and Drafting'. As the title suggests, this book could easily have been written as two volumes. After some debate it was decided to combine the related skills of legal writing with drafting in one book by setting out the common general principles before focusing on the issues specific to the particular skill. The book is therefore divided into three chapters. Chapter One deals with the general principles of legal writing and drafting. Chapter Two covers written communications, such as letters, reports and memoranda. The whole of Chapter Three is devoted to drafting.

The book has been designed to meet the needs of both those who wish to read about the subject generally and those who wish to dip into particular sections, as the need arises. Readers in the former category, who read the book from cover to cover, will discover some repetition, while others with more particular interests will occasionally find the need to cross-refer to other sections. I have tried to strike a reasonable balance between these twin evils. Whilst the tabulated examples I have given illustrate and conform to the rules contained in the text, the text itself is laid out according to the publisher's house style.

GROUND RULES, COMMON SENSE AND COMMON PRACTICE

In some cases, the older hand may object to a suggested rule, approach or convention on the grounds that it does not accord with his practice or his experience of practice generally (which often amounts to the same thing). When describing established conventions (and my own preferences) I have tried, wherever possible, to avoid being prescriptive by pointing out that each firm has its own way of doing things and, in firms where there is no established house-style, the same may be true of individual practitioners. This is an unfortunate truism that makes systematic training problematic and life in general for the trainee difficult. However, just as the aspiring musician must first learn the scales before beginning to improvise, so the beginner needs ground rules for legal writing and drafting. I have therefore attempted to set out those ground rules.

The correct approach for most readers will be to follow a convention or suggestion in this book unless it is in conflict with the preferences of the relevant college, university, firm or principal. Each reader should conform to the expectations of those who assess his or her work as a student or employee but retain an open mind. The hope is that students and trainees will evaluate the strengths and weaknesses of the styles they see in articles and, in time, determine their own style based on merit rather than tradition or habit.

Newcomers and seasoned practitioner alike may agree (although not necessarily on the same issue), that the book occasionally does no more than articulate common sense. This I am happy to concede but the real question is 'is it common practice?' A graduate just embarking on a legal career may be surprised by the mammoth, unpunctuated sentences and antiquated, stilted phrases still used by practitioners today. Practitioners, some of them not so seasoned, seem to forget very rapidly just how little they knew on entering the profession and therefore the areas in which a trainee is in need of guidance.

PERSONAL STYLE AND SENSITIVE ISSUES

Writing is highly stylistic and everyone should develop his or her own style. Whilst I am hopeful that I have eliminated one or two of my more irritating writing mannerisms, I have resisted the temptation to sanitise my style of all its peculiar features. For example, generations of school children were taught that it is bad style to begin a sentence with 'because' or a co-ordinating conjunction such as 'but' and I know from experience that, for some, such an offence is seriously disturbing. But Gowers readily agrees that these words may be freely used in this way and many authors do so to great effect. I have therefore allowed myself an occasional 'But' or 'Because' at the risk of incurring the wrath of some of my readers.

Another highly sensitive area is sexism and the gender of pronouns. It is often alleged that the traditional usage of the pronoun *he* in a generic way, to include both males and females, is a form of sexist writing. In a statute, the draftsman (I cannot accept 'draftsperson' or 'drafter') may rely upon the Interpretation Act or, in the case of a private document, the Law of Property Act. Not so for the solicitor writing a letter and still less for the author of a book on legal writing. A commonly employed answer to the problem is to use a neutral plural word such as 'they' and I have done so where the context permits. But indiscriminate use of this device can lead to other problems. For example, The Law Society's Legal Practice Course Board, in the Introduction to its Written Standards, states:

'The student should be able to:

... demonstrate an awareness of the limits of their own competence and know when to ask for assistance.'

The singular sense of 'The student' should be matched by a singular pronoun rather than the plural 'their'. Of course, if the subject had been the plural 'students' there could be no objection to the use of the sexually neutral 'their'. However, there are occasions when this solution does not work and to persist would be both awkward and extreme. In such cases I have tended to opt for the traditional 'he' where the subject is the villain but otherwise to stick to the safe, if cumbersome, 'he or she'.

'EXCLUSION CLAUSE'

The examples contained in this book are advanced either as instances of bad practice or style or as illustrations of a particular point made in the text. They are not intended to be and should not be used as precedents for your own legal writing and drafting. Whilst you can apply the principles contained in this book to any legal writing task, you should always research the law thoroughly, refer to appropriate forms and precedents and select the words you use with great care according to the particular circumstances.

LAST WORD

Several of the examples of bad habits and common errors cited in this book come from my own writing. Although I have learnt many lessons as a result of researching and writing this book, I readily acknowledge the ample room for improvement. All suggestions will be welcome.

In the meantime, I can only hope that I have escaped the particular ignominy Julie Burchill referred to in an article which appeared in *The Sunday Times* shortly after I agreed to write this book. She wrote,

'Perhaps the hardest thing to write about without coming across as a complete and utter twit is writing itself'.

Chapter One

Plain English and the General Principles of Legal Writing and Drafting

1.1 PREPARATION

Good writing is clear thinking on paper. It has its foundation in thinking, planning and organisation.

We tell ourselves that we do not have the time to plan. Preferring the comfort of knowing the task is underway, we resolve to face the difficulties as they arise (or leave them until last) rather than square up to them from the outset. The result is likely to be a confused and disjointed document, following a less than logical order and not easily understood by our intended readers.

Planning and organising material will force you to address difficulties at an early stage, save considerable revision time and produce a clearer, more readable document.

Before you start writing you should consider:

(a) your aims,

(b)   your readers, and

(c)   how you plan to organise your writing.

1.1.1   Aims

The first step in preparation is to identify your aim. If there are several aims, you should sort them into priority order. You may find it helpful, in an appropriate case, to state your aims in the introduction of your letter or in the recitals of an agreement.

In order to establish your aims you may find that you need to clarify matters. This may involve discussing the task with the partner or other lawyer supervising your work, your client, or others, such as regulatory bodies. This is an important aspect of preparation and will save you time (and possibly embarrassment) later.

1.1.2   Who are your readers?

Forming a strong image of your readers before you begin helps to sharpen your focus and develop a structure for your writing. The better you know your readers, the better your chances of communicating clearly.

To obtain a clear picture of your readers, it may be helpful to ask yourself:

(a)   Who are my readers?

● Can I expect them to understand technical or specialised terms?

● Are they lawyers and if so are they specialists in the relevant field?

● Are they senior or junior?

● Is English their first language?

(b)   What will they need to know?

● What do they know about the subject?

● What information do I need to give them?

(c)   What action is required?

● What steps have to be taken?

● What do I want my readers to do? If you want your readers to act on your writing, make sure the action you require or recommend is clear.

(d)   How is my writing to influence their thinking or behaviour?

● What interests or motivates them?

● Are there other arguments or points of view that need to be addressed?

● What would persuade them to my view?

The first rule of legal writing and drafting is to begin by thinking and to keep thinking about the needs of your reader. You should acquire the habit of writing every letter and drafting every document as if your client, or other intended reader, is watching over your shoulder. It would also be prudent to become conscious of the court, or other tribunal, lurking over the other.

1.1.3   Planning before writing

1.1.3.1   Why plan?
Planning and organisation are the key to effective writing. You should always plan before you start writing to help you develop a logical order and prevent you from repeating yourself or leaving out important information. Your plan will also enable you to edit your document before you write it. When writers fail to plan, they frequently waste much time and effort in editing irrelevant or unnecessary text from a finished draft. It is much easier and less time-consuming to delete it at the planning stage.

Many people resist the discipline of planning on the grounds that it imposes a rigid structure that restricts the evolution of ideas. This is nonsense. Your plan merely represents a record or snapshot of your thinking at a given stage, providing you with a point of reference. It should help focus and organise but not obstruct or inhibit your thinking and writing.

A plan is perfectly capable of being dynamic. It is not necessary to stick rigidly to your original plan and you are free to modify it as you investigate and research your supporting materials. Having a structure before you commence your research helps to shape your thoughts, but you should not allow it to dictate your final draft. It may be that as you research background information you find there are new important points to include or that you must change direction in some way. Far from presenting obstacles, your plan will assist you by enabling you to see how these changes affect other material you have already written or plan to write.

1.1.3.2 The key steps in planning

Your plan may be no more than a few notes jotted on a scrap of paper, e.g. prior to writing a short letter to a client or drafting a general endorsement on the back of a writ. More complex matters may require something more elaborate. Whatever the task, the key steps in developing a plan are:

(a)   Write, in note form, all your ideas that spring to mind concerning the task in hand. Do not, at this stage, attempt to structure them, e.g. in terms of their relative importance or chronological order. Concentrate on recording all your thoughts on the matter, trying to make them as comprehensive as possible.

(b)   Now highlight the main ideas or themes: those that seem appropriate as major headings.

(c)   Transfer your main headings to a new page and enter keywords concerning facts, rules, principles, arguments and examples.

(d)   Decide upon the logical sequence of the items under each main heading, assigning subheadings where appropriate. If a heading appears to have a daunting number of items under it, consider breaking them into separate further headings. This will force you to think hard and logically about your subject-matter.

(e)   Review your plan for relevance by referring to your defined aims and your assessment of your readers and their needs. Delete all irrelevant material and consider the value of retaining non-essential items.

(f) Number the headings in the order you intend to present the material.

1.1.3.3 The order of your material

Your decision as to the most suitable order is important because it controls and influences your readers' approach to thinking about your subject.

Of the many ways to order writing the most common are:

(a) chronological order: setting out the sequence of events,

(b) categorical order: information sorted under categories,

(c) ascending order of complexity: simplest first,

(d) descending order of importance: the most important first;

(e) ascending order of importance: most important last.

Perhaps the most popular with lawyers, particularly litigators, when dealing with largely factual material, is chronological order.

Categorical order is popular with commercial lawyers in relation to complex commercial transactions because it allows readers to move back and forwards through the document with ease and without missing important information. A contract will generally adopt categorical order, particularly in relation to main headings and clauses, often using chronological order within subheadings and clauses where the sequence of events is important. In any event, a contract should follow the order the reader will expect and find natural.

Lawyers often use ascending order of complexity where a client's understanding of the most complex issues will be assisted by a prior understanding of the more straightforward issues.

Descending order of importance is most often used when giving advice where it is important to draw the client's attention to the most important issue or those which will govern his or her understanding of the material that follows.

You can use ascending order of importance to good effect in persuasive writing where you invite your reader to conclude in your client's favour.

1.2 LAYOUT

Layout is not the responsibility of your secretary: it is yours. The appearance of your writing, whether a letter, memo, contract, will or deed, can contribute significantly to the enthusiasm of your readers, to their chances of receiving a clear unambiguous message and to the impression you make on behalf of yourself and of your firm.

Layout can aid readability Most readers are unaccustomed to large blocks of text and will find them unappetising. Many will give up before they reach the end. The reader who perseveres, is likely to lose concentration. Even a momentary lapse can cause the eye to jump several lines of text. This is all the more likely when the same key expression appears regularly. Sensible and consistent use of simple layout devices can help.

Layout can provide a guide to meaning If used well, layout can provide a guide to meaning. If used incorrectly there is a danger that you may mislead the reader. Inconsistent layout may cause your reader to make connections where none were intended, e.g. where separate points appear related because they feature under the same heading, in the same paragraph or indentation.

Layout can help to create a polished impression Never underestimate the power of presentation. The impact of a well (or badly) laid-out document can create a significant and lasting impression of the writer and of the firm.

1.2.1 Some guidelines

1.2.1.1 Line spacing and indentation
Spacing between lines can often make seemingly indigestible text more appetising and is a simple but effective way to make it more readable. Indenting successively, but not excessively, will aid a reader's eye. But beware. If there are more than four levels of indentation readers may have difficulty in keeping track, causing them to leaf backwards and forwards

merely to establish the rank or status of a paragraph. At best you risk annoying your readers and, at worst, confusing them.

1.2.1.2 Margins and white space

Use margins to present your text as a picture in a frame. Leaving white space around the edge of a page and between paragraphs improves the presentation of a document. It makes reading a more attractive proposition and creates a good first impression.

1.2.1.3 Size of print

Use clear typeface in legible sizes. Varying the size (upwards not downwards) can aid readability in the same way as indentation and the same caution applies. As with all layout devices, use should be consistent.

1.2.1.4 Emboldening and underlining

Prudent and consistent use of emboldening, or underlining to show the rank or importance of headings or text can have a considerable effect on a document's readability. However, its overuse can be self-defeating since its currency devalues the more you use it.

1.2.1.5 Tables and columns

Tables and columns can be very useful for presenting large volumes of material in abbreviated form (often falling short of complete sentences). The reader may be able to see on one page the interrelationship of ideas, facts and figures, which might otherwise require several pages of text to express and much leafing backwards and forwards to read.

1.2.1.6 Headings

The use of headings is probably the most powerful layout device available to aid the readability of your document. Use headings liberally if they are accurate and helpful descriptions of sections of text. Be careful not to overcrowd your writing when you add headings. Leave ample space between headings and sections of text to enable them to stand out as signposts for the reader's eye

1.2.2 House style

The most important rule with the layout of documents is: ensure that you are consistent both internally, in relation to the layout of a particular document, and in your writing generally. Clients may become accustomed to the layout of your writing and the good impression you may have made may be damaged by later documents that depart from it.

Many firms have developed a form of 'house style' as a standard to which all documents prepared in the name of the firm should adhere. The benefits are many:

    (a)   The firm presents a 'uniform style' to clients and other solicitors.

    (b)   Typing and amendment of documents is easier and more efficient because all secretaries are trained to use a common format.

    (c)   Training is facilitated by a common standard.

    (d)   It is easier to detect and prevent errors.

    (e)   There is greater automation of standard-form documentation, making production quicker and more cost-effective.

It may be that your firm has developed its own house style. If so you should adhere to it wherever possible (any reservations you may have, other than with glaring errors, may be best saved until you have a degree of seniority within the firm). If your firm has not yet developed a house style, your life as a trainee may be all the more awkward. You may have to adjust your drafting style to that of the partner or other lawyer supervising your work at the relevant time. Your best course may be to find some examples of his or her drafting. Try to distil the prevailing ground rules but actively seek guidance where there appears to be doubt.

Failing adequate guidance on layout it is suggested that you develop your own 'house style' at an early stage. Many of the advantages stated above for firm-wide house style apply with equal force to one adopted by an individual. Your clients are more likely to appreciate your drafting, you should find that documents become easier and quicker to draft, your secretary (becoming accustomed to the format) will type it more rapidly, and there will be fewer errors in the first draft and those that do arise will be easier to spot. In time the conventions you have adopted may help your firm to develop it own house style.

1.3 SENTENCES AND PARAGRAPHS

The basic rule in the construction of a sentence or paragraph is that there should be unity of thought and clarity of expression. If, when writing a sentence or paragraph, you allow yourself to wander from one idea to another there is a significant danger that your reader will become confused. A reader will certainly become irritated with your writing and less inclined to be influenced by what you say. Two or more disconnected ideas require separate sentences or paragraphs.

1.3.1 Sentences

1.3.1.1 The lawyer's tendency towards long sentences
The long sentence is the hallmark of the lawyer. For hundreds of years, English lawyers have had a fixation with long, complicated sentences, beginning before English had developed a uniform system of punctuation, but persisting long afterwards. Lawyers' instincts are to anticipate all foreseeable events in giving advice and drafting documents. This is proper within reason. The main problem is that we have a tendency to express them all in one mammoth sentence. To our accustomed eyes there seems nothing wrong with these epics but, to others, these long sentences make legal writing hard to understand. It is not uncommon to find sentences of 250 words or more in legal documents. Try taking one of your longer efforts, or sample a lengthy clause from a precedent, and read it aloud at normal speed. Then, once you have resumed normal breathing, place yourself in the reader's shoes and ask yourself what it means. As with the spoken word, in legal writing, it is permissible to pause for breath.

1.3.1.2 The problem with long sentences
The average sentence length in business and official writing is high. In contracts, government regulations and legal correspondence averages of 45, with sentences of 60 words or more, are common. Whether this is necessary or justifiable is in part dependent upon the supposed sophistication and experience of the intended reader. However, it is inescapable that, whoever the reader may be, the more words you put in a sentence the harder it is to understand. To sustain a lengthy sentence your grammar will usually have to be complex and unfamiliar. Since sentence structure can be just as puzzling as esoteric words, the reader may not know what the sentence is about until the end approaches.

Imagine the purpose of the following example is to explain the nature and central distinguishing feature of an elephant to a person who has never seen or heard of an elephant:

> An elephant, a species of proboscidean mammal, of which only two now survive (the mastodon and the mammoth long being extinct): the Asiatic (the average adult measuring 2.7m high and 3 tonnes in weight), in India, which may be domesticated and used as a beast of burden, and the larger (6 tonnes) and fiercer African, both sexes of both species having large ivory tusks, of considerable value, is the only animal in the world to possess a trunk.

With a sentence like this, there is only so much that a reader can absorb in one go. The average reader may feel lost halfway through and forget how the sentence started. Most readers will have to read it at least twice to find the meaning. Why make it difficult? Consider the following example:

> An order for an interim payment may be made, provided the Master or District Registrar is satisfied that the defendant has admitted liability, or that the plaintiff has already obtained interlocutory judgment with damages to be assessed, or that if the action went to trial, the plaintiff would be awarded, after deduction of any contribution likely for contributory negligence, 'substantial' damages, and in the present case £25,000 is likely to be regarded as 'substantial', under RSC Order 29 r. 11.

One of the problems with this sentence is that it is like a Russian doll. It opens to reveal a smaller Russian doll that opens to reveal a yet smaller Russian doll and so on. It is difficult to follow because the reader's mind must store each new piece of information in parenthesis until the end of the sentence.

The remedy for a sentence like the one in the example above is to break it into two or three by taking some of the information in parenthesis and putting it in separate sentences.

> A Master or District Registrar may make an order for an interim payment under RSC Order 29 r. 11. He may do so provided the plaintiff satisfies him that the defendant has admitted liability, or that the plaintiff has already obtained interlocutory judgment with damages to

be assessed, or that if the action went to trial, the plaintiff would be awarded (after deduction of any contribution likely for contributory negligence) 'substantial' damages. In the present case he is likely to regard £25,000 as 'substantial'.

The sentence has been rewritten as three sentences. The gaps between subject, verb and object are shorter with greater use of the active voice.

1.3.1.3   Keep sentences short

It is generally recognised that the single most effective way to aid understanding is to use short sentences. In addition, keeping sentence length short will help to avoid punctuation and grammar faults.

There can be no hard-and-fast rules with sentence length but as a general guideline you should aim at an average of 25 words or less. This does not mean that every sentence must be no more than 25 words. Occasionally you may need a longer sentence in which to join two or more closely related ideas. In such a case consider whether using a colon or semicolon would be appropriate.

Average sentence length may be adjusted according to your assessment of the likely readership. A document intended to regulate dealings wholly between business entities might appropriately have an average of sentence length of 29 (this is the approximate average for *The Times*); whereas a contract for a banking client but intended for consumers might aim at an average closer to 23 (the approximate average for the *Daily Express*). However, do not think that, just because your work is for commercial and financial clients, you are necessarily justified in using lengthy sentences. The *Financial Times* consistently manages to maintain a lower average sentence length than its 'quality' rivals despite the technical nature of much of its writing.

1.3.1.4   How to shorten sentences

The best technique for keeping your sentences short from the outset, is to make only one main point in each sentence. In particular, try to avoid non-essential qualifications to the main point in the same sentence. This is a difficult discipline for a lawyer, because it goes against the grain, but it will help .

Even so, it is likely that some unnecessarily long sentences will creep into your writing and need to be edited later:

(a)   Select a paragraph and measure the sentence length. Count the number of words from one full stop to the next, treating hyphenated words and groups of symbols as one word. Do not count citations.

(b)   You should always try to edit sentences with over 40 words, even if you have decided your readers are likely to be relatively sophisticated. If you remember that sentences should generally contain only one main idea, you should be able to divide most long sentences into two or more sentences.

(c)   Be ruthless and cut any words or phrases that add little in support of your main point in the sentence. These are superfluous, however good you think they sound. They devalue your sentence.

(d)   Delete all redundant words and phrases (see 1.7).

(e)   Do all or any of these if it leads to greater clarity even if it requires the use of a few extra words overall.

Sometimes, particularly when drafting, there may be no alternative to a long sentence. In such a case a tabulated sentence may be the answer (see 1.4.5).

1.3.1.5   Vary sentence length

Sentences can be too short and the short-sharp effect can be overdone. Writing in uniform short sentences may lack rhythm and flow, sound abrupt and monotonous and annoy or bore the reader.

Good writing has a natural sounding rhythm that rises and falls. You can create this by varying the length and rhythm of your sentences, balancing longer sentences with shorter ones to achieve the desired average sentence length.

1.3.2   Paragraphs

A paragraph is either:

(a)   a grouping of a series of sentences connected with the development of some single idea or dealing with some single subject, or

(b)   a single sentence that alone conveys that idea or deals with that subject.

At the planning stage you will have arranged your material under main and subheadings. These may themselves equate with appropriate paragraph breaks. If they contain several themes, separate each theme into a paragraph of its own. Never attempt to explain more than one theme per paragraph.

Properly used, paragraphs will help you to achieve two objectives. They will aid comprehension by separating one theme from another. They will also provide a natural pause for the reader's mind to absorb and reflect upon one theme before embarking on the next.

Large blocks of unbroken text are always unappetising and often indigestible. It is better, wherever possible, to write in 'bite-sized chunks'. The longer the paragraphs the sooner the reader may tire, become confused or even give up. If the paragraphs are short, readers can control their own pace and concentrate on each main point of the document more easily. In addition, however complicated or difficult the material, short paragraphs make documents look easier to read.

1.3.2.1   Average paragraph length
A good rule of thumb is that paragraphs should on average be less than six sentences long. As with sentences, the length of a paragraph will largely be determined by the complexity or importance of the theme and your assessment of the likely readership of the document. A minor subject will usually call for only a brief paragraph: a major theme may demand a longer one. You may wish to adjust the target for your average paragraph length according to the likely readership for each document. It is important to grasp that the target is an *average* of six. Naturally, some paragraphs will need to be longer.

By way of contrast, a one-sentence paragraph can be very effective to gain the reader's attention or to make a key point.

When testing your writing for over-long paragraphs, bear in mind that the shorter your sentences, the higher your average for paragraph length. If your score on sentence length is a good one you should not be too concerned about the average for paragraphs. However, you should check that you are keeping to one main theme per paragraph.

1.4 PUNCTUATION

It seems strange that the idea of good punctuation as crucial to good writing, a fact universally recognised outside the legal profession, has only just begun to be acknowledged within the legal world.

1.4.1 Historical background

Traditionally lawyers have drafted documents with little or no punctuation. It is often asserted, in defence of this practice, that, until the mid 19th century, Acts of Parliament were deliberately passed unpunctuated in the interests of precision. However, research by leading academic writers suggests that punctuation can be found in the earliest of statutes, albeit erratic in its application.

A more plausible explanation lies in the practices of the early printers. There being no common standards or conventions it was common for printers to change the punctuation in documents to conform with their personal style. Lawyers could not be sure that their documents would be printed with the punctuation they intended or that the punctuation in a statute was as it was enacted. As a consequence, they construed statutes and other documents without reference to their punctuation and made a skill of drafting documents supposedly capable of being understood without it.

1.4.2 Modern judicial interpretation

The case for ignoring punctuation was supported by *Sanford v Raikes* (1816) 1 Mer 646) in which Grant MR said at p. 651: 'It is from the words, and from the context, not from the punctuation, that the sense [of a will] must be collected'.

This passage was cited with approval, albeit *obiter*, by Lord Westbury in *Gordon v Gordon* (1871) LR 5 HL 254 at p. 276. However, by the time the issue came before the House of Lords in *Houston v Burns* [1918] AC 337 a more standard approach to punctuation had been adopted by publishers and printers. Lord Shaw of Dunfermline said:

> Punctuation is a rational part of English composition, and is sometimes quite significantly employed. I see no reason for depriving legal

documents of such significance as attaches to punctuation in other writings.

The court, then, will have regard to punctuation in construing a document, although it will disregard it if it runs counter to its otherwise plain meaning.

1.4.3 Lawyers' excuse for omitting punctuation

The supreme irony is that lawyers, the writers of the longest sentences known to man, have claimed to construct them without the aid of punctuation in the interests of precision. Everyone else uses punctuation precisely because it is an invaluable guide to meaning. Computer programmers, for whom syntactical precision is crucial, even use it in their languages.

The advocates of sparse punctuation seek to justify the practice on the grounds that punctuation can be misleading. This, of course, is true. Incorrect or inconsistent punctuation can have disastrous consequences. Roger Casement is said to have been 'hanged by a comma'. But this is an absurd argument. Using words incorrectly can mislead, but nobody would seriously suggest we should not use words. The solution is simple: lawyers should use punctuation but use it correctly and consistently.

1.4.4 Some guidelines

Punctuation marks are like traffic signals to your readers. They provide rhythm, telling your readers when to pause, slow down, stop and go on. Using too many commas and too few full stops are the most common punctuation problems. If you keep your sentences short you will avoid many errors in punctuation. When you use a long sentence avoid peppering it with unnecessary commas or leaving out commas altogether. If in doubt, try reading your writing aloud so you can hear if the stops and pauses occur naturally.

Apart from the basic rule, that every sentence begins with a capital letter and ends with a full stop, it is difficult to lay down many fixed rules for questions of punctuation. The following can only be regarded as guidelines to the correct use of punctuation. These guidelines incorporate some of the standard practices relating to punctuation used by printers and publishers, which in the absence of contrary 'house style' conventions may help in cases of doubt. For a discussion of incorrect use you may wish to refer to Fowler's *Modern English Usage* under the heading 'stops'.

1.4.4.1 *Capitals*
Apart from the well-known rules that capitals are used to begin a new sentence, to introduce a quotation, for proper nouns and the name and day of the month, Fowler says their use is largely a matter of taste. I suggest the following:

(a)   Capitals are appropriate for full titles of persons, ranks, officers, institutions, countries, buildings and books – whether general or particular, singular or plural.

(b)   When referring to institutions, bodies and the like by use of an abbreviated form of the name, the use of a capital initial is permissible, e.g. 'Commissioners' for 'Commissioners of Inland Revenue'.

(c)   Sometimes a capital letter is conventionally used to distinguish one meaning of a word from another, for example, 'State' (organised community), 'state' (condition). However, this distinction is often unnecessary because the meaning is clear from the context.

To lay persons it may appear that lawyers regularly compound their failure to adhere to any recognised set of guidelines by littering their writing with seemingly random capitals. The unconventional use of capital initials in legal documents to highlight defined words is discussed in 3.12.1.1.

1.4.4.2 *Commas*
Fowler gives a comprehensive list of the misuses of the comma. Here are some instances of its correct use:

(a)   A comma is primarily used to insert a pause into a sentence so as to break it up into articulate phrases or clauses. The test, when inserting a comma into a sentence of two or more clauses, is to read the whole sentence, noting where the voice naturally pauses.

(b)   Commas may operate as a form of parenthesis in the same manner as a pair of dashes or brackets and must then come in pairs. The trap with using commas in this way is that it is easy to open the parenthesis with a comma but fail to spot the omission of the closing comma. For example:

> A counter-notice must be given to the landlord, who may, or may not, be the immediate landlord who served the notice terminating the tenancy and must be given within two months of the landlord's notice.

The reader is left either in suspense, continuing to read in expectation of a closing comma, or in ignorance, not realising that the words following the comma were intended to be in parenthesis. The passage should have read:

> A counter-notice must be given to the landlord (who may, or may not, be the immediate landlord) who served the notice terminating the tenancy and must be given within two months of the landlord's notice.

In a short sentence, the reader may be able identify the error and easily adjust the meaning. In a typical contract clause it may cause, at best, irritation at having to scroll backwards and forwards until the fault is located and the sentence deciphered. At worst, it may be misconstrued with serious consequences for you and your client.

(c)   Commas are used to separate words of the same type in a list of three or more items, or to separate a series of phrases or clauses. Commas can be particularly important when listing given names and surnames. Consider the clarity of the following:

> David John Samuel Barry Stuart Martin Patrick Douglas Timothy James Edwards and Peter Peters, (the 'Directors').

Although attacked by some as illogical, it is now generally accepted practice to omit the comma before the words 'and' or 'or' in a series unless including it would add clarity.

(d)   In reported speech, to mark a person addressed, a comma is inserted before the person's name, e.g.

> 'Let him have it, Chris.'

> 'I agree, your honour.'

(e) A comma is usually inserted after a phrase that begins with a present participle (-ing), e.g.:

Opening the plaintiff's case, he began his speech.

(f) A comma is used to mark off such words and phrases as: 'therefore', 'however', 'of course', 'for instance'.

1.4.4.3 Semicolons
The semicolon, a longer pause than a comma, separates complete clauses, or quasi-sentences within one sentence. Their use will enable you to avoid three problems in writing: the abruptness of a series of short sentences; the monotony of a long sentence consisting of clauses strung together with 'and' or some other conjunction; and the confusion of a complicated sentence divided only by commas. Semicolons may be used:

(a) To separate coordinate clauses when conjunctions, especially 'and', are omitted.

(b) In enumerations consisting of predicate phrases or clauses (not single words) dependent on the same subject and main verb, e.g.:

She said that she was now always tired; in constant pain; physically less mobile; unable to continue in her work.

(c) To separate long clauses dealing with the same subject, when a pause longer than that indicated by a comma is required, especially when commas have already been used in the individual clauses. This can help to avoid the use of an otherwise unduly long and unmanageable sentence.

(d) To separate two coordinate clauses, particularly where the second begins with a conjunction (moreover, nevertheless, otherwise, therefore) developing an idea contained in the first, e.g.:

You must acknowledge service of the writ; otherwise the plaintiff will enter judgment in default.

This helps to present a more cohesive statement than the alternative of using two separate short sentences.

A semicolon is not followed by a capital letter.

1.4.4.4 Colons
Colons are used:

(a)   To add a sentence or phrase to another sentence or phrase, such as a conclusion or deduction which follows from the premise of the first phrase.

(b)   To introduce a list (but not where the list is simply the object of a verb, e.g. 'He sued the owners, their agents and employees').

(c)   To introduce a summary to a statement, e.g.:

'The position is as follows: the defendants have an arguable case, they are likely to pay into court and obtain leave to defend.'

(d)   To introduce a quotation (a comma is increasingly used for the same purpose, particularly where the quotation is short).

(e)   To separate two balancing halves of a complete thought, e.g.:

'Man proposes: God disposes.'

1.4.4.5 Brackets
Brackets, properly used, are equivalent to a footnote. They facilitate the insertion of an aside which is necessary if the substance of the sentence is to be fully understood. Although a pair of commas or dashes can provide an alternative, brackets have the advantage: they always come in pairs whereas dashes and commas do not. The reader will know the significance of the first bracket on reading it. This will not necessarily be true of the first comma or dash.

In the interests of clarity, brackets are best avoided where one phrase is to be contained within another bracketed phrase. It is preferable to use commas, dashes or quotation marks for the inner phrase.

Square brackets are used when, within a quotation, unquoted material is to be interjected, e.g. by way of précis of original material or explanation.

1.4.4.6 Dashes
Generally a dash is considered useful for the purpose of marking hesitation, e.g. 'I – er – think . . .'; parenthetical interruption; abrupt aside

or afterthought; introduction to a passage of explanation; amplification; gathering up the subject of a long sentence and the spring of a surprise or whimsical ending of a sentence.

1.4.4.7 Hyphens

According to Fowler, the infinite variety of usage for the hyphen defies description: no two authorities give the same advice. For practical typographical purposes it is used to show the continuation of a word divided to maintain a right-hand margin. The primary purpose of the hyphen, however, is to indicate that two or more words are to be read together as a single compound word with its own meaning, e.g. jury-box. Notice the difference between, 'the best known remedy' and 'the best-known remedy'.

1.4.4.8 Quotation marks

Quotation marks are used to enclose the spoken word, a quotation from or the title to a book or other publication and to indicate a foreign or unusual word. Practice varies. Fowler prefers to regard single quotation marks as of general application resorting to double marks only for quotations within quotations. This is also Blackstone's convention and it is adopted in this book.

1.4.4.9 Apostrophes

An apostrophe is used to show the possessive, e.g. 'the defendant's solicitor'. In the singular possessive the apostrophe comes before the 's' as in 'the defendant's evidence' or 'the administratrix's case', even where the singular word ends in 's', e.g. 'St James's'; 'Delors's'. This rule is usually not followed when the last syllable is pronounced '-iz', as in 'Moses' law' or for ancient classical names such as Euripides. There are further exceptions where the normal rule would pose a problem for the spoken word, e.g. 'Achilles' heel'; 'Pears' soap'.

In the case of plural possessive the apostrophe comes after the word and the 's' is usually omitted as in 'publishers' proofs' and 'witnesses' statements', including plural names that take a singular verb, e.g. 'Reuters''; 'Barclays''; 'Salomon Brothers''. The ''s' ending is used after plurals that do not end in 's', e.g. 'children's'; 'media's'. Trying to make a possessive form of 'Lloyd's' (of London) is problematic and should be avoided where possible.

For a few words it is necessary to use 's to make a plural. This should be done only if it is required to make it clear that the 's' is to produce a plural, e.g. it is not required in 'the three Rs', or 'the 1980s', but it is required in 'the three I's'.

An apostrophe can also be used to indicate the omission of one or more letters as in 'can't' for cannot. Do not fall into the trap of writing 'it's', unless you mean the contracted form of 'it is'. The possessive of 'it' is 'its'. Similarly, never use an apostrophe in other possessive pronouns, e.g. 'hers'; 'ours'; 'yours'.

1.4.5 Tabulation

Sometimes there really is no alternative to a lengthy sentence. Often the best and clearest solution is to retain the use of a single sentence but to present the material using introductory words followed by a list. This is known as a tabulated sentence.

It is sometimes necessary to continue a tabulated sentence beyond the list with some concluding words. Since readers may experience some difficulty relating the end of the sentence to the introductory words or the words in the list, it is preferable to avoid the use of concluding words wherever possible.

When you tabulate a sentence you should:

(a) only include items of the same class;

(b) make sure that each item is consistent, in substance and in grammar, with the words appearing before the colon and any words following the listed items;

(c) begin each item with a letter or number;

(d) use successive indentation where appropriate; and

(e) place a semicolon after each item except the last, followed by either:

(i) 'or', if the list is disjunctive, or

(ii) 'and', if the list is conjunctive

Where the list and all the individual items are sufficiently short so that the reader will not become confused and all the items in the list are either exclusively disjunctive or conjunctive, you may omit the 'or' or the 'and' after each semicolon except the one following the next-to-last item. For example:

> Our client also claims for reimbursement for the following items of loss and damage:
>
> (a) hospital fee of £310.70;
>
> (b) telephone calls totalling £3.40;
>
> (c) insurance excess and loss of no claims bonus at £210;
>
> (d) towing charges of £70.50;
>
> (e) cost of repairs to the vehicle at a total of £753.32; and
>
> (f) cost of alternative transport for a period of three weeks at £115 per week.

The use of several sentences would probably have resulted in unnecessary repetition of words such as client, claim, reimbursement, loss and damage or their synonyms.

Lawyers are quite used to using tabulation in drafting but many seem reluctant to do so in letters. Consider the following example.

> Whilst your planned expenditure would be wholly and exclusively incurred for business purposes, your sales promotion ideas may fall foul of a specific provision in the Taxes Act concerned with business entertainment expenses unless they come within one of the exceptions. The expenditure will be deductible if the items are not provided by way of gift but supplied under a contract collateral to a contract of sale; or provided by way of gift and are either goods other than food, drink, tobacco or vouchers exchangeable for goods costing you less than £10 per customer and carrying a conspicuous advertisement for your

business; or goods which it is your trade to provide for payment; and you give them away with the object of advertising to the public generally.

If the second sentence is tabulated it becomes easier to read and understand.

Whilst your planned expenditure would be wholly and exclusively incurred for business purposes, your sales promotion ideas may fall foul of a specific provision in the Taxes Act concerned with business entertainment expenses unless they come within one of the exceptions. The expenditure will be deductible if the items are:

(1) not provided by way of gift but supplied under a contract collateral to a contract of sale; or

(2) provided by way of gift and are either

(a) goods other than food, drink, tobacco or vouchers exchangeable for goods

(i) costing you less than £10 per customer; and

(ii) carrying a conspicuous advertisement for your business; or

(b) goods which

(i) it is your trade to provide for payment; and

(ii) you give them away with the object of advertising to the public generally.

Tabulation can also be useful where you wish introductory words to apply to two or more complete sentences. Begin each sentence with a capital letter and end it with a full stop.

1.5 SENTENCE CONSTRUCTION AND GRAMMAR

1.5.1 Constructing and editing with 'telegram' words

There are two kinds of words in every sentence: 'telegram' words and 'link' words. The message of the sentence is carried by the 'telegram' words. The purpose of 'link' words is to connect 'telegram' words so as to give them particular and unambiguous meaning by forming them into a grammatical sentence. If the ratio of link words to telegram words is too high the sentence will seem heavy and cumbersome. It will be hard to find the message buried beneath a pile of unnecessary words.

Legal writing is much criticised for being too 'wordy' or verbose. Constructing your sentences from 'telegram' words can help to keep your writing crisp and your sentences short. It is also a good practice to keep an eye on the ratio of 'telegram' words to 'link' words when editing sentences.

It will help the construction of your sentences if, before you begin writing, you sketch out the sentence in telegram form. This approach is really an extension of the planning process. It will enable you to see the best way to construct your sentences to convey your meaning.

When editing a 'wordy' sentence, isolate the telegram words and reorganise the sentence with fewer link words. It is undesirable, and probably impossible, to lay down a strict rule as to the optimum ratio. A ratio of 1 to 1 will produce a tight, terse sentence ideal for forms, procedures, most internal memoranda and letters of record, but too impersonal to be appropriate when writing to clients. However, it is recommended that you do not exceed a ratio of three link words to each telegram word. The optimum will lie between these two ratios, depending upon the nature of the document and its intended readership.

In the following unnecessarily long piece the telegram words have been underlined:

> Now that the defendants in your action have admitted liability, there is another aspect of this case that requires your consideration. It may be possible in the circumstances to obtain an order from the court that an interim payment be made in relation to pecuniary loss, in advance of the action being actually heard *in toto*. For this purpose, would you please write or call at your earliest convenience to confirm that what you have lost financially is as we have set out in a letter, a copy of which we enclose herewith.

In all <u>likelihood</u> the <u>defendants</u> will <u>agree</u> to making an <u>interim</u> <u>payment</u>. In the event of the defendants' <u>refusal</u>, we intend to make an <u>application</u> to the <u>court</u> for an <u>order</u> that such a payment be made. It should be noted that, for these purposes, we shall require you to <u>swear</u> an <u>affidavit</u> 'verifying' your abovementioned pecuniary <u>loss</u>. Meanwhile, as a basis for this, we should like your confirmation of these facts, and also for you to <u>send</u> to us <u>all forms</u> or <u>papers</u> you may have received <u>from</u> the <u>DSS</u> or from your <u>employers</u> relating to <u>benefits</u> you have <u>received</u> over the <u>last three months</u>, and also your <u>wage slips</u> for the same period.

Here is the same piece with the links rewritten:

Now that the defendants in your action have admitted liability, it is probable that they will agree to pay you a proportion of your loss prior to the hearing. If the defendants refuse, we intend to apply to the court for an interim payment order.

In order to do this, we will need you to swear an affidavit 'verifying' your financial loss. Please confirm by letter or telephone that your losses are as we have set out in the enclosed letter and send us all forms or papers you may have received from the DSS or from your employers relating to benefits you have received over the last three months and your wage slips for the same period.

1.5.2 Subject (actor), verb (action) and object

Another way to avoid poor construction or remedy a 'wordy' sentence is to follow the normal order of subject-verb-object. A sentence must have a subject (stated or understood) and a finite verb (i.e. limited in number and person by the subject). It will often, but need not, contain an object (the sufferer of the action).

Construct or rewrite your sentence by asking yourself:

Who/what is doing what to whom?

Then:

(a)   State the subject or the actor.

(b) State the action by using the strongest available verb.

(c) State the object of the action (if there is one).

The reader, seeking the meaning of a sentence, will search for the subject, the verb and the object. If they are set out in that order and in close proximity the reader will readily understand. Unfortunately, not only do lawyers have a tendency to write lengthy sentences, they frequently force readers to make vast leaps from the subject to the verb and from the verb to the object. This was the essential problem with the 'mammoth sentence' in 1.3.1.2. The reader had to leap 65 words from the subject to the verb. The best way to narrow so wide a gap is to remove the intervening words and convert them into separate sentences.

Where the gap is between the verb and the object the same problem arises.

> The relevant accounting standard provided that, if an offeror obtained at least 90 per cent of the fair value of all equity shares in the offeree as a result of the offer but held less than 20 per cent immediately before the offer was made and at least 90 per cent of the fair value of the consideration was in the form of equity share capital, an acquisition could be accorded merger accounting treatment.

With this example, the best solution is to move the intervening words to the end of the sentence:

> The relevant accounting standard provided that an acquisition could be accorded merger accounting treatment if an offeror obtained at least 90 per cent of the fair value of all equity shares in the offeree as a result of the offer but held less than 20 per cent immediately before the offer was made and at least 90 per cent of the fair value of the consideration was in the form of equity share capital.

More often, where the gap between verb and object is excessively wide, the intervening words are better placed in separate sentences.

1.5.3 Correct grammar

Writing can be grammatically correct yet difficult to read. This book focuses on communication as the root of good legal writing rather than

concentrating on correct grammar. Obviously, good grammar is important to legal writing but most communication problems are not caused by
grammatical faults. Writing may have grammatical faults yet convey its
message.

Unfortunately, there is much disagreement about rules of English
grammar. Even where there is agreement the rule is often subject to
numerous exceptions. The truth is that failure to observe the rules,
whether from ignorance or for convenience, does not usually affect
meaning.

It is not suggested that you abandon or ignore grammatical rules. Quite
apart from questions of form, to do so runs the risk of alienating your
readers. There are many who regard the rules as of first importance,
placing great value on one rule over another. I was once astonished to
read an internal memorandum at one firm in which the managing partner
publicly berated another partner at great length over his use of the
expression 'meet with' in the minutes of a meeting – a phrasal verb which
was allegedly, amongst other things: 'an unnecessary and vulgar
Americanism'. His objection was, perhaps, a valid one but his reaction
seemed to be out of all proportion with the offence and the opportunity
cost of the time expended. Nevertheless, he was a very important and
influential figure within the practice and not the sort of person with whom
many partners relished debate, still less young trainees. If you are aware
of partners and other senior lawyers in your firm for whom grammatical
rules are paramount it is as well to take heed.

Even if you (and the solicitor supervising your work) are relaxed about
these rules your readers outside the firm, including your clients, may not
be. For example, the rule against split infinitives (e.g. 'to never split' or
'to boldly go') remains implanted in many readers' minds.

It is therefore best to avoid splitting an infinitive unless, as sometimes
happens, doing so would lead to ambiguity. For example, the need to
position a modifier so as to avoid ambiguity should override the
grammatical rule not to split an infinitive. If the sentence:

Part of your job as a solicitor is to really understand your clients'
problems

is reconstructed to avoid the split infinitive its meaning becomes ambiguous:

> Part of your job as a solicitor is really to understand your clients' problems.

Wherever possible you should adhere to the rules but you should not allow worries about grammatical intricacies to cloud other principles of clear writing. Since there is much controversy, the choice of one form over another should not lead to serious consequences. In any event, by following the guidelines in this book you will find it harder to make grammatical errors, e.g. if you maintain a low average sentence length and use active verbs you are less likely to use incorrect grammar.

1.5.4 Avoiding negatives (and double negatives)

The use of a positive phrase is usually preferable to a negative because it is more direct and is usually shorter. If a negative expression is unavoidable, beware of the dangers of piling up the negatives: the grammar may be correct but the construction may be an ordeal for your readers causing them to perform mental somersaults as they read. It is also easy to fail to spot your own mistakes, e.g.:

> I should not be surprised if delivery is not delayed by at least two weeks.

The sense you intended was:

> I expect delivery to be delayed by at least two weeks.

Unfortunately, the meaning of what you wrote was:

> I expect that delivery will *not* be delayed by at least two weeks.

This applies not just to negative words such as 'not' and 'none' but also to words which use prefixes such as 'non-', 'un-' and 'il-' and other words that can operate in a negative way, such as 'fail', 'terminate', 'void', 'cancel', 'except', 'unless' and 'other than':

The court held that it was for the bank to show that the company had *failed* to take *insufficient* care.

The writer intended:

The court held that it was for the bank to show that the company had *failed* to take *sufficient* care.

In letters or memoranda, the error is usually the result of writing by extemporary dictation into a dictaphone followed by a failure to check properly. The best way to avoid this kind of mistake is to use positive expressions where possible and to make rough notes before you begin writing.

If you find that you have written two or more negatives in the same sentence:

(a)   Identify each negative.

(b)   Cancel two negatives by pairing them: this should produce a positive.

(c)   Rewrite the sentence using the positives.

1.6   WORDS AND PHRASES

Your purpose in writing is primarily to communicate. So write to express not to impress. As with so many aspects of writing, your choice of words should be determined by your assessment of your likely readership. Here you have an advantage over most writers. Lawyers can usually form a fairly accurate picture of their likely readers and should be able to select the most appropriate words.

1.6.1   Unfamiliar words

Unfortunately, many lawyers have acquired the habit of using complex or unfamiliar words where simple everyday ones would do. They think it sounds more important and provides a learned tone. Do not fall into this trap. Not only does this habit add unnecessarily to the length of your text, too often it also serves to obscure the message causing your readers to reach for the dictionary or skip the words without understanding them. This is as much your loss as theirs. Clients and others are impressed by good advice clearly expressed, not by writing shrouded in mystery.

Naturally, there will be occasions when the use of complex words is unavoidable. Sometimes, particularly with technical words, there will be no alternative but to use an unfamiliar word. But, given a choice: choose the familiar. Use 'send' instead of 'forward', 'notify' for 'give notice' and 'under' for 'pursuant to'. For more examples see the Undesirables Checklist in the appendix 1. Preserve the reader's attention and stamina for when you need to use technical words to convey precise meaning.

1.6.2   Technical words

Sometimes the use of unfamiliar words is unavoidable where they have a precise technical legal meaning. For example, in conveyancing, it would be inappropriate and unwise to depart from words such as 'fee simple', 'trust for sale' or 'conveyance'. In a will, you might use the expressions 'residue' or 'testamentary expenses'. But do not make this an excuse for lazy drafting. The expression 'devise and bequeath' is commonly found in wills. Both words mean 'give'; 'devise' being more appropriate for land and 'bequeath' for other types of property. In many cases you can choose either 'devise' or 'bequeath' without consequence. Better still, delete them both in favour of 'give' in *all* cases.

Once you have decided to use a technical legal expression, it will need no definition in a formal document such as an agreement, will or conveyance. This does not mean that the term should be left unexplained. Never assume that your clients (or others who will need to understand your writing) understand these technical legal words. You should consider the likely readership and decide whether a particular expression calls for some guidance. This may be contained in a letter, or in guidance notes where you or your client foresee regular reference being made to it, e.g. reference by personnel managers to contracts of employment, and pension or share option schemes. In some documents, particularly consumer contracts, you may need to provide some guidance in the contract itself.

When drafting documents regulating commercial transactions it is sometimes appropriate and convenient to incorporate the terminology of the particular trade, business or profession, e.g. in international trade agreements the expressions 'f.o.b.' and 'c.i.f.' have established meanings and the courts will have no difficulty in ascertaining the intentions of the parties where such expressions are used.

However, you should exercise extreme caution. Do not incorporate a phrase unless you are quite sure you know how that expression is understood in the relevant business and that it is sufficiently precise to be an aid to drafting. Be particularly careful with accountancy terms, e.g. 'off balance sheet financing'. It will often be tempting to use expressions used by your client or other advisers to the transaction when you are not absolutely sure you understand them. Never assume that you can gather their meaning from the context. For all you know they may have been misused.

Beware also of business jargon used as if it has a precise meaning when it is capable of several different shades of meaning. For example, 'MOF' was a popular expression in the commercial banking world in the late 1980s broadly meaning a facility under which banks would undertake to provide a wide range of options for raising debt finance all in one agreement. Because banking clients used it as a useful shorthand lawyers tended to pick it up as though it had some legal significance when in truth it was no more than a catchy label for a novel marketing idea.

If you are left in any doubt about a term either avoid using it or regard it as a useful abbreviation and provide a definition which sets out precisely how it is to be understood in the particular transaction.

1.6.3   Jargon

The word 'jargon' describes a common language of specialised terms used within a group of experts or professionals which (though not technically precise in the sense of having a statutory, judicial, scientific or other established definition) can, if used sensibly, be useful within these groups.

A lawyer writing to another does not have to explain the expression '*res ipsa loquitur*'. It would be highly unusual not to use such shorthand. It would add unnecessarily to the text and perplex the other lawyer, causing him or her to search for some subtle reason for the departure from the expression they both understand. On the other hand, to use terms such as these when writing to a client might be seriously puzzling.

If through some non-legal expertise you may have (e.g. scientific) or through years of advising clients from a particular industry or sector, you are acquainted with specialist terms, use them when writing to the client if doing so aids understanding and precision.

However, dangerous confusion and misunderstanding can result when jargon is used outside these groups. It is very easy to fall into the trap of writing in jargon. It is a comfortable and lazy way to write but it rarely helps the reader. The more specialised you become as a lawyer the greater the likelihood you will develop a jargon habit. When you write for people outside your specialist field (including other lawyers), take special care to ensure that they will understand the words you use. Keep jargon to a minimum, and explain it by using definitions, examples or illustrations. Never attempt to use jargon to impress or intimidate your readers.

1.6.4 Abbreviations

Abbreviations can operate as a form of jargon, convenient for experts in the same field, confusing for others. Sometimes, lawyers compound the problem by abbreviating jargon. For example, 'ADR' may have no meaning to one reader, it may mean 'American depository receipt' to another and a third reader may think it means 'alternative dispute resolution'.

However, used sensibly, abbreviation can be a useful device to help your readers. Use an abbreviation when you need to use an expression repeatedly and its repetition may irritate your readers or add excessively to the text. See 3.12.2.

1.6.5 Abstract words

Lawyers are naturally cautious and instinct tells us to provide for every foreseeable possibility and, even then, to leave an escape route for the unforeseen. When drafting or writing on your client's behalf this is a skill for which your client is paying. Intentionally vague words like 'reasonable' in 'use reasonable endeavours'; or 'material' in 'disclose all material facts', are often used when the draftsman does not wish to be limited to the presently foreseeable.

This can be overdone. You can be over-protective of your client causing unwarranted delay, obscuring the commercial purpose of the transaction and frustrating the parties' willingness to bargain. The extent to which you use these devices should be governed by the facts of each case. You should not allow them to creep into your writing as a matter of habit.

In particular you should resist the temptation to use abstract words when giving advice. Lawyers love abstract words like 'situation', 'basis' and 'circumstances'. This seemingly impressive camouflage can conceal vague and evasive expression. Unfortunately, clients are not impressed at all. One of the most commonly expressed frustrations with lawyers is that it is difficult to tie them to a definite view. Clients want clear specific advice unfettered by 'weasel words'. Wherever possible be specific and avoid hiding behind abstractions. For example, the writer of the following letter is sheltering in abstractions:

The defendants, through their solicitors, have now notified us of the fact that they have made a payment into court in the sum of £3,750 in full and final settlement of your claim.

In a payment-in situation you have 21 days in which to accept the sum or proceed to trial and run the risk that the award made is the same as or less than the sum paid in. In such a case the plaintiff will have to pay the defendant's costs.

We are aware of the fact that this sum falls short of your original aspirations. However, you may recall that we were in agreement concerning a minimum sum to be accepted by you. It will be noted that the amount paid into court is in excess of that figure and that, having had the benefit of conference with counsel, you will be fully appraised of the weaknesses of your claim.

Accordingly, subject to your confirmation, we are proposing to accept and draw out the sum now in court. Please write to us at your earliest convenience to confirm, so that we may go ahead well before the time when the offer will be withdrawn.

Since you have been in receipt of legal aid, the said sum will be subject to the statutory charge and will not be paid out to you until costs have been taxed and deducted.

In view of the above, we would advise you to accept the offer.

Now the same letter rewritten in more direct terms:

> The defendants, through their solicitors, notified us today that they have paid into court the sum of £3,750 in full settlement of your claim.
>
> This means that you have 21 days in which to accept this sum. If you decide not to accept it the case will proceed to a hearing. The judge will have no knowledge of the payment during the trial but, if you win the case and the award is no greater than the sum paid in, the court may require you to pay the legal costs the defendants incur from now until the end of the trial.
>
> We are aware that this sum is less than you hoped for. It is, however, more than the figure we agreed with you as the minimum you should accept and, given the views expressed by counsel as to the strength of your case, we would advise you to accept the offer.
>
> Please write to us as soon as possible if you wish to accept the offer so that we may draw the sum from court well before the end of 21 days. As you have received legal aid, the money will be paid into the Legal Aid Fund and remain there until all the costs of bringing this case have been recovered. The costs have to be 'taxed' or approved by the court. As this procedure could take six months or more, we would ask the legal aid authorities to release part of the sum to you on our undertaking that the claim for costs will not exceed the remainder.

1.6.6   Foreign words and phrases

The use of Latin and Law French by lawyers may have historical roots but it has no justification in modern practice. At best it is an affectation turned to habit, at worst, an attempt to intimidate the reader. These foreign words and phrases have English equivalents which are every bit as good and more likely to be understood. For example you never need to use '*inter alia*' because you can always replace it with 'among other things' or delete it. Straying into a foreign language is not a good way of writing plain English. Nevertheless the words you choose to use should be a matter of individual judgment in each case and much depends upon your assessment of your reader. For examples of foreign words which are best avoided see the Undesirables Checklist in the appendix.

There are two reasons why you should avoid these foreign words and phrases. The first is that they belong to a language with which you may have little or no acquaintance. As Fowler puts it, with these words, 'lurk unsuspected possibilities of exhibiting ignorance'. In one firm the expression '*éminence grise*' (meaning 'confidential agent' or 'one who exercises power unofficially') was used by a partner to describe a new information technology strategy for the firm. One individual seized upon the phrase enthusiastically, evidently thinking it meant 'superiority' or 'importance', and misused it repeatedly in internal memoranda and in the minutes of numerous meetings. Use foreign words at your peril.

Although you may know how to use a foreign word correctly, the second reason why you should not use it is that you cannot be sure your readers will understand it. Many people do not understand expressions such as '*inter alia*' or '*pari passu*'. Confronted by an unfamiliar foreign expression they may ignore it altogether or hope to find the meaning from the context of the sentence. This is no way to convey your message.

1.7 AVOID REDUNDANT WORDS AND PHRASES

1.7.1 Redundant words and expressions

One effective way to shorten your sentence length and make your writing more readable is to make every word count by cutting out redundant phrases. These are the unnecessary phrases we all find ourselves using which could be replaced with a single word or deleted altogether with no loss of meaning.

The desire to emphasise a point can sometimes result in tautologies (see later) and other redundant words. For example, 'must necessarily'. If it is necessary that something be done, it must be done. The word 'duly' is usually redundant. It means 'properly and punctually' but the expression is often used unnecessarily where a thing is either done or not done and no time has been set for performance.

Your meaning will not become clear by adding the word 'clearly' or 'obviously'. If your message is already clear, 'clearly' is redundant. If what you say is obvious it might be better not to say it at all. Similarly, you cannot expect to influence your reader's assessment of the relevance or significance of something by saying, 'It is important to add that'. Your readers will usually infer that you regard it as important from its inclusion. Whether they agree with you will depend upon how well you express your argument.

1.7.2 Compound constructions

Compound constructions use three or four words where a simple form of words would use one or two. For example: 'with respect to the lease', 'with regard to the lessor', and 'so far as the lessee is concerned' can be shortened by beginning the sentence with 'Concerning' or 'Regarding'. However, it is usually better to delete the expression and restructure the sentence.

The expression 'for the reason that' can be replaced with a simple 'because' and 'the fact that' is nearly always redundant in all its forms. You should also regard phrases containing words like 'case', 'instance' and 'situation' with suspicion. For further examples of redundant expressions that you can delete with no loss of meaning see the Undesirables Checklist in the appendix.

1.7.3 Clichés, overused words and mixed metaphors

1.7.3.1 Clichés
To some, clichés are stale phrases that have lost their original impact through overuse. To others, they are powerful precisely because they are hackneyed. It would be wrong to say that you should never use a cliché. Sometimes its use in a novel context can produce freshness to an otherwise hackneyed expression. Use a cliché if it is the best way to say what you mean.

The danger with clichés is that they provide prefabricated phrases that can become tired substitutes for original thought. They have a nasty habit of suggesting themselves as we write. If you begin to write 'alliance', somehow 'unholy' might slip in or if there is an 'irony', it might easily become a 'bitter' one without your giving it much thought. Used with care, an occasional cliché will not harm your writing. If you use one, use it because it expresses your meaning clearly and not simply because it is familiar.

1.7.3.2   Clichéd antique formulas

Victorian clerks developed a style of writing which contained a catalogue of stilted formulas. Unfortunately this practice became so ingrained by the turn of the century that you will still occasionally come across writers who believe that the use of these formulas is a mark of good business writing. Their letters will be filled with old-fashioned and formal expressions, e.g. 'at your earliest convenience', 'enclosed herewith'. For more examples see the Undesirables Checklist in the appendix. Do not copy these standard phrases in your writing. They are generally regarded as outmoded and unsuitable in modern business and they will ruin the natural flow of your writing.

1.7.3.3   Overused words

Inexperienced writers often overuse words that sound impressive to try to make their message sound more important than it is. These may be 'vogue' words: words that emerge from obscurity (or legitimate specialist language) into sudden popularity. At first you may be aware that you are using one of these words but their use soon becomes a habit. By this time the words will have lost their novel impact. For example: 'actual', 'meaningful', 'nice', 'phenomenal', 'terrible' (which can usually be deleted without losing any meaning), 'interface', 'materialise' and 'syndrome' (which will require replacement with a more specific word). For more vogue words see the Undesirables Checklist in the Appendix. Take care not to overstate your case by overuse of these words. Compare:

The actual result was that the defendant lost the case,

with:

The result was the defendant lost the case.

1.7.3.4   Overused metaphors

Use metaphors in technical or legal writing only as a last resort. Some of the more overworked or misused metaphors like 'blueprint', 'bottleneck' and 'catalyst' are included in the Undesirables Checklist in the appendix. For a more detailed discussion refer to *The Complete Plain Words*.

1.7.4 Tautologies, qualifying words and overemphasis

1.7.4.1 Tautology

Tautology is the repetition of the same idea in different words in the same phrase or sentence. If your writing contains phrases like: 'combine together', 'forward planning', 'important essentials', 'past history', 'mutual cooperation' and 'new innovation', it suggests that you are not thinking clearly about what you want to say.

Some tautologies like 'blend together', 'condense down'; and 'revert back' are harder to resist, but once you become aware of them in your writing it becomes easier to eradicate them from your style.

1.7.4.2 Qualifying words and overemphasis

Qualifying words can be overused. When we wish to emphasise a point words like 'absolutely', 'completely', 'really', 'totally', and even 'very', appear when they are inappropriate. Once identified you can delete them without losing any meaning. For example:

Counsel's advice *totally* convinced me that a change of tactics was *definitely* needed

is improved without loss of emphasis by deleting the qualifying words:

Counsel's advice convinced me that a change in tactics was needed.

Similarly, the word 'very' is often best deleted. For example:

My client is *very* determined to appeal this decision

is better as:

My client is determined to appeal this decision.

Writers who use these qualifying words excessively find that they lose their effect. If everything ordinary is 'absolutely' or 'totally' or 'completely' it becomes difficult to describe accurately the genuinely unusual or exceptional.

When you wish to give your writing special emphasis, select a stronger or more descriptive word that needs no qualification, rather than qualifying a neutral or moderate word. For example:

The plaintiff's claim was totally unrealistic

is better as:

The plaintiff's claim was absurd.

1.7.4.3 Qualifying an absolute

The careless use of qualifying words can also produce embarrassing tautologies. Qualifying words should never be applied to absolute words like 'unique', 'true' or 'unanimous' if you intend to describe an absolute state. To say 'more' or 'less' or 'completely', 'unique', 'true' or 'unanimous' is contradictory and meaningless. However, if you qualify the expression to describe something falling just short of an absolute, although it will irritate the purist, it will not produce a tautology, e.g. 'almost unique', 'nearly unanimous'.

Qualifying words should be used with care and in moderation. Keep a lookout for overemphasis in your writing and delete unnecessary qualifying words. If you save them for the occasions when they are essential, the qualifying words you do use will have greater emphasis.

1.7.4.4 Redundant legal pairs

Legal tautologies are words of identical meaning, grouped in pairs or even triplets, where only one is necessary. For example, in the expression 'null and void', 'null' adds nothing to 'void' and 'void' nothing to 'null'. Lawyers of the 'belt, braces and bicycle clips' school will cautiously add 'totally' to 'null and void'.

'Last will and testament' loses nothing as the simple 'will'. Although 'suffer' in 'suffer or permit' has a slightly different meaning to its partner 'permit', it is a word that has long outlived its life in ordinary usage. 'Permit' alone would seem to suffice in most, if not all, cases.

Legal pairs are often defended on the basis that they are terms of art which promote certainty and precision. However, whilst it may occasionally be true to say that one word in a pair has a slightly different shade of meaning to the other (e.g. suffer and permit), pairs are often used when that difference can have no consequence. In any event, the niceties claimed are illusory when the differences have ceased to be recognised in common usage for a century or more.

Legal pairs are far from being terms of art. A term of art is an expression that has an accepted meaning and which, by its compression of language, creates economy with words. An expression such as 'hearsay' is an example. But expressions like these are used between lawyers for rapid communication of ideas, they are not used in drafting. Further, far from achieving compression of language, legal pairs cause repetition.

Try to avoid using these worthless expressions in your writing.

1.7.5   Archaic language

'Legalese', like 'aforementioned', 'whereas', 'hereinafter' and 'said', gives legal writing a musty Dickensian air but rarely adds anything of significance. Unfortunately, lawyers often use these archaic phrases quite needlessly. This is largely a result of the traditional training system and the unquestioning habit of many lawyers. Instinctively, lawyers will seek to justify their use of these old expressions claiming that they are in some way more precise than ordinary modern English. This argument does not withstand close examination. When used in drafting these expressions create a false impression of precision when in reality they conceal lazy thinking. The use of legalese in correspondence, particularly with non-lawyers, is unforgivable.

Why should a lawyer's words differ from the words used in ordinary English? Apart from statutory or judicially defined words and terms of art, there can be no justification for a word used only by lawyers when it has a modern equivalent in common usage.

For examples of archaic words and how to avoid them see 3.16.2.

1.8   VERBS: ACTIVE AND PASSIVE VOICES

1.8.1   What are active and passive verbs?

When you use a verb in the active voice, the subject of the sentence is the agent that *performs the action* and comes before the verb. For example:

The judge (subject/agent) interrupted (active verb) the defendant's counsel (object).

The defendant (subject/agent) served (active verb) a defence (object).

The subject of the sentence is *acted upon* when you use a verb in the passive voice. A passive verb enables you to place someone or something other than the agent first in the sentence, in the position of the subject. For example:

The defendant's counsel (subject) was criticised (passive verb) by the judge (agent).

A defence (subject) was served (passive verb) by the defendant (agent).

1.8.2 Why prefer the active to the passive voice?

The following table summarises the characteristics of the active and passive voices:

Active	*Passive*
personal style	official style
simple, easy to read	ponderous, heavy to read
informative and specific	evasive and vague
clear and precise	ambiguous
direct	indirect
short sentences	long sentences

The main advantage of using active verbs is that they force you to be specific and direct. When using the active voice, it is impossible to leave out the agent in a complete sentence. You cannot say:

authorised and signed the cheque.

Even where the passive form supplies the same information, the active is usually preferable. For example:

The cheque was authorised and signed by the finance director (passive voice).

The finance director authorised and signed the cheque (active voice).

The passive version uses more words. In the active voice, the words 'authorised and signed' suffice. In the passive voice, they need 'was' and 'by' to support them.

The most serious objection to the passive voice is its potential for ambiguity. When using passive verbs it is possible to write sentences that omit the identity of the agent. A sentence truncated in this way may withhold information needed by your readers:

The cheque was authorised and signed (no expressed agent).

The truncated passive style of writing is attractive to lawyers because it allows them room to manoeuvre. There will be occasions when, for legitimate reasons (see 1.8.5), you may wish to omit the agent in a sentence. However, it is important that you do not do so through habit. Unthinking use of the passive voice in legal writing can be dangerous. You should be particularly careful where you contemplate someone taking some form of action. If you use the passive voice it may be unclear who is to perform the action.

1.8.3 How to identify passive verbs

Passive verbs are not always easy to identify in your own writing. However, the first rule to remember is, in the active voice, the subject is also the agent performing the action of the verb. The passive voice reverses the sentence order with the subject receiving the action.

It may also help to know that passive verbs always use a form of the verb 'to be' before the past participle of another verb. Most past participles are easy to spot because the majority of them end in 'ed'. For example, 'leveraged', 'questioned', 'signed' and 'talked'. So, joining one of the forms of the verb 'to be' with a word of this type produces a passive verb. For example:

is	authorised
are	blamed
was	created
were	divided
be	evaded
been	formed
being	hired

This model agreement is intended to illustrate the typical events of default we have recommended for a term-loan agreement entered into by Megan Bank (passive).

This model agreement illustrates the typical events of default we recommend for Megan Bank term-loan agreements (active).

1.8.4 How to make passive verbs active

You can convert a passive voice to an active one either by placing the agent before the verb or by changing the agent of the verb.

1.8.4.1 Place the agent before the verb

To place the agent before the verb, locate the verb and determine who or what is performing the action. For example:

The defendant's counsel was interrupted by the judge (passive).

Take the verb 'interrupted' and ask yourself 'Who did the interrupting?' The answer is 'the judge'. Place the agent, 'the judge', before the verb, 'interrupted', and rewrite the sentence as follows:

The judge interrupted the defendant's counsel (active).

1.8.4.2 · Change the agent of the verb

Sometimes you may find that rearranging the sentence by placing the agent before the verb does not provide a satisfactory solution. The answer is usually to change the agent and rewrite the sentence. For example:

When the goods were delivered they were found to be faulty (passive).

Here the agent of the verbs 'were delivered' and 'were found' is unstated – perhaps it is the buyer of the goods. Placing the agent before the verb produces an unsatisfactory result:

When the buyer took delivery of the goods he found them to be faulty.

The sentence is still in the passive voice and the emphasis may be wrong. If the writer's message is not that the buyer took delivery of the goods or that he inspected them but that the goods were faulty then the better approach is to change the agent to the seller:

The seller delivered faulty goods (active).

By changing the agent from the buyer to the seller the verbs become active and you direct the reader's attention to the alleged breach, not to the less relevant actions of the buyer.

1.8.5 When to use passive verbs

The most important legitimate use of the passive voice is where it is better not to state the agent of the verb.

1.8.5.1 The agent of the verb is unknown, self-evident or irrelevant
For example:

The goods were stolen in transit (passive).

This may be a legitimate use of the passive. First, the writer may not know who stole the goods. Although it is usually possible to contrive an agent, e.g. 'The thief stole the goods whilst they were in transit', the result is pedantic and often tautologous. Secondly, the identity of the thief may be irrelevant. Your readers may not need to know who stole the goods to understand the message you wish to convey. The use of the passive voice is therefore used correctly where the thing done or to be done is important and the person or other agent performing it is not. This will frequently be so in technical writing. For example,

To satisfy the limitation period in personal injury cases the writ should be issued within three years of the accident.

This passage would be legitimate in a text book but not in a letter to a client who not only wants to know when the writ should be issued but also who is going to do it.

In many cases, the identity of the agent is also self-evident. 'A defence was served' is usually better than 'The defendant served a defence'. Here the passive with an unstated agent is preferable to the active voice because it is self-evident that it was the defendant who served the defence. It seems likely that the important message is that the defence was served rather than the identity of the person who served it.

1.8.5.2 It is important to emphasise the object of the sentence rather than the subject
This arises where you want to focus attention on the receiver of the action. For example:

No record of the company was found at Companies House (passive).

I carried out a search at Companies House but I found no record of the company (active).

The reader's interest is the absence of records at Companies House. Here the passive voice enables you to focus the reader's attention on the object where it is more important than the subject.

1.8.5.3 You want to avoid giving specific information or giving the impression of being critical
By deliberately using the passive you avoid identifying an individual and divert attention from the subject towards the object. For example:

An error was made in calculating your redundancy pay (passive).

The head of personnel made an error in calculating your redundancy pay (active).

The potential legal consequences of this breach are serious and should not be allowed to happen in the future (passive).

The finance director should never do this again (active).

1.8.6 Be human

Gowers's exhortation to all writers to be human, quoted in the introduction, is never more apt than when applied to legal writing. Lawyers too often ignore people and address their message to some remote abstraction. The use of the active voice helps to avoid what one writer has termed lawyers' 'cosmic detachment'.

Law in action always involves people. Even the mightiest corporate client acts through people. You aim to influence their thinking and conduct by your writing. When turning passive verbs into active verbs you need to ask yourself 'Who is doing what to whom?' Be prepared to bring these people, including yourself or your firm, into your sentences and detachment and abstraction will fall away. Above all, remember that your principal aim is to communicate and that your reader's needs are paramount. Sensible use of the word 'you', or your reader's name, will make your writing more personal, encourage you to use the active voice and enable your readers to understand more clearly the impact of your message upon their lives and the steps, if any, they should take.

1.8.7 An example

In the following example, the passive voice is used 16 times.

> We refer to the medical report prepared on our client, Mr M. Lingerer on 19 March 1993.

> Please be advised that it has not been possible to agree the medical evidence and attendance at the hearing will therefore be required. A subpoena will be issued by the court. Your expenses will be reimbursed. Details of actual loss of income incurred by you should be sent to us so that the maximum amount payable can be duly remitted to you.

> With regard to the date of the hearing, the action will be entered in the 'Warned List' in approximately six weeks' time and it is estimated that the case should be heard on or about the week beginning 9 May 1994. Final notice of the day actually fixed for the hearing will only be received by us on the Friday of the week before but you will be notified as soon as possible thereafter.

> A statement of your evidence is enclosed herewith. A copy of the report of Mr Newall, the opponent's medical expert, which has been supplied to us by the other side, is also enclosed. A meeting will be arranged with your secretary to discuss this report and the questions likely to be asked of you at court.

Now here is the same letter rewritten with the active voice except in two places where the unstated agent is either self-evident or irrelevant. Some clichés and archaisms have been removed.

Our Client, Mr M. Lingerer: Medical Report 19/3/93

We have been unable to agree the medical evidence in this case. The court will therefore send you a subpoena requiring you to attend the hearing. Please let us know, in due course, the loss of income you incur and we will ensure that you are reimbursed.

We expect the case to enter the 'Warned List' after approximately six weeks and we estimate the case will be heard on or about the week beginning 9 May 1994. The court may notify us of the day fixed for the hearing only on the Friday of the week before, but when we know the date we will contact you immediately.

We enclose a copy of your statement of evidence together with a copy of a report prepared by Mr Newall, the opponent's medical expert, which solicitors for the other side have supplied. We should like to discuss the report with you and your reactions to the questions counsel for the defendant is likely to ask. We therefore plan to call your secretary over the next few days to arrange a convenient appointment.

1.8.8 Concealed verbs

Another way to use verbs more effectively is to use base verbs rather than concealed verbs. This will shorten your sentences and makes your writing more direct. Concealed verbs are verbs converted into nouns. Unfortunately, when many lawyers write, judges no longer 'decide', they 'make decisions' and parties are not required to 'pay', they must 'make payment'. If you use these clumsy derivative nouns you will find that you need surplus words to support them.

For example:

The parties reached an agreement to make a settlement (concealed verb).

The parties agreed to settle (revealed base verb).

It may be of some assistance if you reach agreement with the other party that an obligation to make payment will be imposed if termination takes place (concealed verbs).

It may assist if you agree that if the other party terminates he will be obliged to pay (revealed verbs with one passive).

... agree that the other party will pay if he terminates (revealed active verbs).

Writers also conceal verbs by placing them between 'the' and 'of', turning them into nouns. For example:

The decision saw the reversal of the effect of many tax-avoidance schemes (concealed).

The decision reversed the effect of many tax avoidance schemes (revealed).

In the verification of a prospectus you must check every detail (concealed).

To verify a prospectus you must check every detail (revealed).

When you find a concealed verb, try to improve the sentence by replacing it with a base verb. This does not mean you should banish all concealed verbs. Sometimes they can be useful to soften an otherwise overly abrupt passage. Rather, you should be careful not to overuse them.

1.9 MODIFYING WORDS

Modifying words add to the meaning of other words. You should exercise care when using these words, ensuring that they modify the intended words and only those words. The classic illustration of ambiguous use of modifying words is the will which features an expression such as:

Charitable institutions or deserving organisations.

Does this mean charitable institutions and any deserving organisation whether charitable or not? Or does it mean charitable institutions and charitable deserving organisations? If the latter is the intended meaning the solution is usually to repeat the modifying word.

A misplaced modifier can produce embarrassing ambiguity. For example:

> The defendant was prevented from building under a little-known by-law.

> We have arranged a conference for you to discuss the implications of your residence in the UK with counsel.

The following sentence illustrates how modifiers can lead to misunderstandings when writing in the passive voice:

> Being clearly incompetent, we take the view that a dismissal is justified in this case.

The main rule with modifiers is to place them as close as possible to the word or words you intend to modify. But some words like 'frequently' and 'often', when placed between phrases, can operate to modify either phrase and therefore require special care. For example:

> A trustee who misappropriates trust funds often cannot be punished.

> Plaintiffs injured in road traffic cases frequently fail to find eye-witnesses.

The solution is usually to place the modifier at the beginning (sometimes at the end) of the sentence.

One modifier with great potential for causing ambiguity is the word 'only'. You could add it to the following sentence in one of eight positions producing a variety of meanings:

> The victim confirmed that he struck her.

If placing 'only' immediately before the word or words you wish to modify fails to cure potential ambiguity, rearrange the sentence so that 'only' is either the first or last word in the sentence and is immediately followed or preceded by the words to be modified.

1.10 REPETITION AND ELEGANT VARIATION

The need to mention the same article or idea several times in a sentence or a paragraph can present a dilemma in legal writing: either use the same word or phrase several times and risk tedium or use synonyms, pronouns or abbreviations and risk confusion.

1.10.1 The golden rule

The golden rule of legal writing and drafting is: be consistent. This dictates that you should:

(a) Never change your language unless you intend to signal a change in meaning.

(b) Always change your language where you intend to signal a change in meaning.

1.10.2 Elegant variation

Invariable repetition of the same word or phrase may promote certainty but it can also produce inelegant and monotonous writing. Elegant variation, a tool of composition taught at school, is the practice of attempting to avoid the repetition of the same word in a sentence or paragraph. Although synonyms can occasionally be used without risk of misunderstanding, careless use can cause dangerous confusion. Attempted elegant variation by the inappropriate use of synonyms and expressions such as 'the same' can produce letters like these:

Re: 888 Constance Gardens

We act for the landlord of the *abovenamed property*, and on his behalf we enclose notice to quit.

The *leased premises* were let to you pursuant to your contract of employment to enable you to carry out your duties and the lease of the *said premises* provides that you will be required to vacate the *demised premises* upon the *cessation* of your employment. Our instructions are that your employment has recently been *terminated*.

We should be glad if you could make arrangements to vacate the *leased property*. If you fail to do so in good time, we are instructed to take proceedings in the County Court for an order for possession of the *said property*.

Re: Account No 5001

We have been instructed by Intelligence Ltd in connection with the *amount outstanding* on your account. According to our client's records the *debit balance* stands at £5,420.56 and no payment has been made in reduction of the *said sum* since a month past.

We would be grateful if you could provide us with your proposals for clearing this *balance*.

Re: 75 No Man's Lane

Your purchase of the *above property* has now been completed and we trust that you have encountered no difficulty in taking possession of the *same*. As you are aware a mortgage has been executed in respect of the *mortgaged property*. This means that the *said property* cannot now be sold without the consent of the *lender*.

We enclose a copy of your mortgage deed and the *building society's* rule book. The documents of title for the *property* are held by the *mortgagee's* solicitors who will proceed with the stamping and registration.

Do not leave your readers to puzzle over non-existent distinctions. If you have chosen the right word do not be afraid to repeat it where necessary.

If there is any doubt the golden rule should prevail. Synonyms and other devices used to mitigate the tedium of repetition are dealt with at 3.15.5. There are, however, more serious pitfalls with repetition.

1.10.3 Dangers of repetition

When the repeated phrase is a lengthy one the writing will also suffer from very long sentences. The conscientious reader will feel obliged to leaf backwards and forwards to compare similar passages and check for subtle differences. Slight unintentional changes will send him or her searching for hidden meanings. On the other hand, slight differences intended to signify subtle changes in meaning may be so camouflaged by repeated expression that they pass unnoticed by the less cautious reader. Even exact repetition can cause problems when used in different contexts. Finally, be careful not to use an expression capable of several meanings in more than one of its senses. This advice may seem an axiomatic rule but it is surprising how often lawyers fail to adhere to it.

1.10.3.1   Slight variance
You should exercise great care when repeating phrases, e.g. first in the recitals and again in the operative part in an agreement. You can cause dangerous confusion if you fail to use exactly the same words. The variance may be interpreted as intentional and the words construed differently.

One of the problems with repetition of long phrases is that the mind tends towards automatic mode when it recognises similar patterns. This is just as much a problem for writers and typists as it is for readers. When checking passages with repeated expressions the author will have a greater tendency than usual to read what he or she expects to read. The omission of one or two words in dictation or typing is easily done but difficult to spot.

If you are satisfied that the best approach in a given case is to use the same basic formulation of words and intentionally introduce variations to convey subtle but significant changes in meaning, make sure that you bring these variations to your client's attention if there is any danger of misunderstanding.

1.10.3.2   Different contexts
You should not automatically assume that a repeated expression will always carry the same meaning when used in different contexts. The context may contribute significantly to the interpretation of an expression.

1.10.3.3   Homonyms: same word – different meaning
It seems ironic that lawyers who set great store by precision of language frequently use words that have more than one meaning. The use of the word in one sense and its repetition soon after in another can be very confusing.

The proposed solution of joining the directors to the subscription agreement gives no consideration to the problem that the promise is not supported by consideration.

The word 'condition' is often used in its general sense, of a term of a contract, and in its technical sense, as a term going to the root of the contract the breach of which amounts to a repudiation. Where the word is used in both its senses in a passage, lawyers may be able to discriminate between the meanings (sometimes not without a struggle). Others may be bewildered.

1.11   USING THE RIGHT WORDS

The English language is full of pitfalls and, without care, it is easy to make the wrong choice of words. There are many words that have the same or a similar sound but different meanings. With certain notorious words, even where, as the author, you may understand these distinctions, you may fail to notice typing errors when checking the draft. This is all the more likely when you are working under pressure to deliver quickly.

A wrong word can distort the meaning of your writing, potentially confusing or misleading your readers. It may also cause clients, other solicitors or your colleagues to question your competence. Never use a word until you are confident that you know its meaning. Before you dictate a word you are unsure of check it in a dictionary and check the draft carefully when it returns following typing.

1.11.1   Commonly misused words

Because of popular misconceptions, some words are more often misused than used correctly. As a result these words should carry a warning to writers to check their meanings if they are to be used with confidence. For example:

We anticipate an offer in settlement within the next week.

This is incorrect: 'anticipate' should be used only in the sense of forestall or foresee and take action against. An example of correct use would be:

We can anticipate the possibility of removal of assets from the jurisdiction by obtaining a *Mareva* injunction.

The word 'dilemma' should not be used as a grand way of saying 'problem' or 'difficulty'. It means an enforced choice between two unfavourable alternatives. For example:

The client's dilemma is that if the company defaults on the loan the bank will enforce the guarantee against him.

This sentence does not disclose a true dilemma. The following is an example of correct use:

The dilemma is that the directors may face serious consequences under the legislation if they continue trading; but to cease trading now may amount to a failure to take the steps required by the same legislation to protect creditors.

The word 'inaugurate' is thought to mean formally to admit to office and not 'start', 'begin' or 'introduce':

The Board should inaugurate changes to company procedures in order to comply with the new rules

is an example of incorrect use. The following example uses the word correctly:

The senior partner gave his inaugural lecture as Visiting Professor of Law at Sorry University.

The word 'refute' should not be used to mean 'deny'. It means 'prove the falsity or error' and is properly used when counter-argument or evidence is present not when there is mere denial.

'Via' is often used incorrectly as a synonym for 'by means of' or 'by'. For example:

Acceptance may be made via post or facsimile.

The witnesses are travelling via ferry and train.

In both these examples 'by' should have been used. 'Via' means 'by way of, or passing through a route or path'. For example:

Appeals usually reach the House of Lords via the Court of Appeal unless the leap-frog procedure is used.

1.11.2 Commonly confused words

It is easy to confuse words that have similar sounds, particularly where they have related but distinct meanings. Some of the most common of these occur through poor dictation or checking, e.g. 'bought/brought', 'quite/quiet', 'its/it's', 'their/there'. Others are more often the result of carelessness, ignorance or both.

Similar words	*Their different meanings*
abdicate/abrogate	*Abdicate* means 'renounce formally an office or power'. *Abrogate* means 'repeal or cancel'.
adverse/averse	*Adverse* means 'opposed, contrary or hostile'. *Averse* means 'strongly disinclined'.
amiable/amicable	*Amiable* means 'agreeable and good natured' and is applied to persons and their dispositions. *Amicable* means 'friendly, peaceable and pleasant' when referring to relationships, arrangements or settlements.
canvas/canvass	*Canvas* is a cloth material. The verb *canvass* means 'to ascertain, discuss and solicit opinion'; the noun means 'a solicitation of support'.
compliment/complement	*Compliment* means (verb) 'to flatter, praise'; (noun) 'a flattering expression'. *Complement* means 'full number of elements for completion'.
effect/affect	*Effect* means 'to bring about' or 'to accomplish'. *Affect* means 'to have an influence on'.

esoteric/exoteric	These are opposites. *Esoteric* means 'intended only for or intelligible only by the initiated'. *Exoteric* means 'intelligible to outsiders'.
forego/forgo	*Forego* means 'go before'. *Forgo* means 'do without'.
infer/imply	*Infer* means 'deduce or conclude' whereas *imply* means 'express indirectly; insinuate'. The distinction lies in who is to do the insinuating and who is to receive it. It is for me to imply my meaning in my writing. It is for you to infer my meaning from my writing.
license/licence	To *license* (verb); a *licence* (noun). In the USA, *license* is commonly used for both.
practise/practice	To *practise* (verb); a *practice* (noun). In the USA, *practice* is commonly used for both.
principal/ principle	*Principal* means 'chief', usually an adjective it may also be a noun, e.g. 'an agent acts for a principal. *Principle* is always a noun and means a 'general law or rule'.
rebate/refund	*Rebate* means 'a deduction from a sum paid or to be paid; a discount'. *Refund* means 'pay back money received from another or reimburse for expenses incurred by another'.
stationary/stationery	*Stationary* is an adjective meaning 'not moving'. *Stationery* is a noun meaning 'writing materials'.

1.11.3 Controversial words

1.11.3.1 First(ly), secondly, thirdly
Many people maintain that the correct way to commence a sequence of points in a paragraph or sentence is 'first (secondly, thirdly)' and never 'firstly', which is condemned as a modern solecism. They argue that

words like 'second' and 'third' are adjectives requiring the suffix 'ly' when they are used as adverbs. To add 'ly' to 'First', which is both an adjective and an adverb, is like saying 'betterly' and 'bestly'.

Others regard the distinction as pedantic and unnecessary preferring firstly as by far the most common usage.

1.11.3.2 'Per centum', 'per cent' or 'per cent.'?

Many regard 'per cent.' as correct, the full stop implying that it is an abbreviation of 'per centum'. But according to the *Oxford English Dictionary* the expression may have originated from the Italian '*per cento*' or the French '*pour cent*', both meaning 'for a hundred'. In either case the expression appears to have been later pseudo-Latinised as 'per centum'. The usage 'per cent' without a full stop is preferable in the interests of simplicity.

1.11.3.3 Spelling conventions

Many words in the English language are capable of being spelt in more than one way and often a particular spelling is more acceptable in a particular context or industry. Be aware of the different possibilities, choose the most appropriate spelling and make a note to yourself (and to your secretary) to keep to it. If you do this, the likelihood of inconsistencies arising will be reduced.

Here are some suggestions:

adviser	not *advisor*
flotation	not *floatation*
judgment	not *judgement*
moneys	not *monies*
movables	not *moveables*
per cent	not *per cent.* or *per centum*

There has long been dispute about whether the verb ending '-ise' should be spelt with a z (as preferred by Oxford University Press) or an s (as preferred by HMSO and the publishers of this book). Given that 'ise' is used in statutory and government publications used by lawyers, it is suggested that it is the one to adopt.

Even though English lawyers are now greatly influenced by American lawyers it is recommended that, where a word has a recognised English spelling as opposed to an American variation, you should use the English spelling. For example, use *adviser* not advisor and *stabilise* not stabilize.

However, it is difficult to generalise about some spellings because usage is changing and sometimes the context is all-important. The American spelling of the English 'programme' is '*program*' in all contexts. However, the reduced spelling has come to be standard in English when dealing with legal issues relating to the computer industry. Similarly, the American '*disk*' is adopted and '*data*' is treated as a singular noun (unlike the traditional usage in the Data Protection Act).

1.11.4 Words of similar sound

It is usually best to avoid the use of words of similar sound and appearance such as 'employer' and 'employee', which tend to make a letter or document difficult to read. You should be particularly careful if you plan to dictate the letter or document because of the danger of a word being misheard by a secretary and the error going unnoticed at the time of checking. The result can be quite disastrous.

In most cases it is possible to use a formulation which is less likely to confuse a reader and which also reduces the chance of error. For example, you could use 'company' and 'employee' in an employment matter; and 'mortgagor' and 'mortgagee' might be translated as 'borrower' and 'lender', in an appropriate case. For 'lessor' and 'lessee' you might use 'landlord' and 'tenant'.

1.12 REFERENCES TO STATUTES, CASES, DATES AND NUMBERS

1.12.1 References to statutes and cases

Generally, statutes are referred to by their short title. When referring to a section in a statute the word 'section' is usually typed in lower case and a reference to a subsection of a section made by referring to, for example, 'section 2(2)'. If it is necessary to refer to a statute repeatedly within a document it is permissible to abbreviate it, for ease of reference, by its initials and year. For example, the Companies Act 1985 may be abbreviated to 'CA 1985'. Common words used in a statute's title are often omitted from an abbreviation, as are any brackets. For example, the Law of Property (Miscellaneous Provisions) Act 1989 may be abbreviated to 'LPMPA 1989'.

The convention with cases is that the case name, but not the citation, is underlined. For example, Re Charge Card Services Ltd [1986] 3 All ER 289. Follow the style of citation used in the law report cited. Most modern reports put the year of publication in square brackets. This indicates that the date is an indispensable part of the reference. With reports which put dates in round brackets, the date is treated as useful but non-essential information, the volume number being of primary importance. You should therefore faithfully reproduce the correct style of citation. For example, (1888) 13 App Cas 523 is the correct citation for Tailby v Official Receiver, whereas the correct citation for Tai Hing Cotton Mill Ltd v Kamsing Knitting Factory is [1979] AC 91.

It is not the publishers' practice to underline cases and this convention is observed in this book.

1.12.2 Dates and numbers

Generally, it is best to state a date by expressing the day in figures, the month in words and the year in figures with no punctuation. For example, '5 May 1993' as opposed to, for example, 'the fifth day of May in the year 1993'. Stating the month before the day is an American practice.

Numbers are best spelt in words up to nine. Beyond this, use figures, unless the number begins a sentence (which you cannot conveniently reconstruct), when it should be spelt. Where the accuracy of a number is vitally important, it is prudent to state the figure in numbers and words. For example:

'£25,000 (twenty-five thousand pounds sterling)'.

Chapter Two

Letters, Memoranda and Reports

This chapter will show how the general principles discussed in chapter 1 are put into practice when writing letters, notes, memoranda and reports.

2.1 PREPARATION

No lawyer, however expert, can produce a perfect first draft. When dictating or writing longhand, most people are capable of only thinking 15 to 20 words ahead. Sometimes, with particularly long sentences, you may have little or no idea how the sentence is to end. As new ideas spring to mind, different words will occur to you. To add to the mayhem, you may have to deal with all kinds of interruptions when in mid-flow. Incoming mail, queries from secretaries, surprise visits from partners and telephone calls from clients, other lawyers, colleagues and friends may distract you from your writing task and disturb your train of thought. If you have attempted dictation without a plan or rough draft on paper, you may have to rewind the tape and listen to it from the beginning to regain an idea of the thread and structure of the letter, report, note or memorandum.

Good legal writing is good legal thinking on paper. It is vital to do all or the majority of your thinking before you start writing. Write only when you know exactly what you want to say.

2.2 LETTER WRITING: AIMS

What is the purpose of your letter?

● Is it to inform?

● Is it to persuade?

● Is it to record?

What do you want your letter to achieve?

● Is a letter really necessary or desirable to achieve your objective?

● Could your objective be achieved better by a meeting or a telephone call?

What do your correspondents need to know and why do they need to know it?

● What do they know about the subject?

● What information do you need to give them?

Select only the information relevant to your reader's needs. Place yourself in your reader's shoes and imagine what you would already know about the document's subject-matter. Think about what you would want and need to know.

What action is required?

● What steps have to be taken?

● What do you want your readers to do?

If you want your readers to act on your writing, make sure the action you require or recommend is clear.

Is your writing to influence your readers' thinking or behaviour?

● What interests or motivates them?

● Are there other arguments or points of view that need to be addressed?

● What would persuade them to your view?

As a general rule, you should aim to ensure that your writing is:

● accurate and complete: otherwise further correspondence will follow, resulting in extra work and loss of time;

● clear and precise: aim to avoid ambiguity and to write in a style that is readily comprehensible;

● contemporary: aim to only use words in modern usage and delete archaic and other expressions;

● short and simple: aim to 'keep it short and simple' – the 'KISS' principle – use short, familiar words and delete redundant expressions;

● polite, human and tactful: aim to be sympathetic, polite, helpful, patient, appreciative, courteous and tactful – never patronising;

● Prompt: aim to write and reply promptly – delays are discourteous and harm the reputation of your firm.

2.3   ORDER

The next stage is to order the material appropriate to your aims. Broadly, there are two types of written message and you need to identify the category into which your writing falls because it should influence the order in which you present your ideas. Writing may be:

(a)   factual, instructional or informative, or

(b)   persuasive, influencing or advising.

2.3.1   Factual, instructional or informative

Whilst most lawyers do not often find themselves writing full factual reports (see 2.9.3 for report writing generally) they regularly write letters that simply aim to provide information or record the happening of events.

The generally accepted technique for reporting factual information is to deliver it in a top-heavy structure which gets the main message across as quickly as possible. Eighty per cent of the information is presented in the first 20 per cent of the report.

Think of your newspaper or of television and radio news broadcasts. Journalists are trained to tell as much as possible, as accurately as possible, in as little time as possible. First comes the headline, there then follows a summary with the essence of the story, then the detail is revealed in stages in descending order of importance.

This is the best way to present a factual report. Your readers will appreciate it because the main points will be available quickly, preparing the way for them to take in the detail more effectively. In a very detailed report, once your readers have read the main points, each can choose how much to read according to his or her purpose in reading.

2.3.2 Persuasive, influencing and advising

The main drawback with the factual report structure is that it can make some letters and reports too hard-hitting. This is especially so if you are seeking to influence someone or persuade a person to accept your recommendations, advice or point of view. For a persuasive letter to succeed you may need a more subtle approach, building towards your recommendations and leading your reader to the same logical conclusion.

Use the 'Six 'P's':

1. Purpose

State the purpose of the letter and what you intend it to cover. If you do this you will provide useful guidance for your reader and a reminder to yourself to keep to the point and exclude irrelevant material.

2. Problem

Outline the problem or nature of the transaction as you understand it.

3. Précis your conclusions

If you précis or summarise your conclusions towards the beginning of the letter your reader will then be able to read the body of the letter with some knowledge of the direction your reasoning will lead. This will aid understanding.

4. Possibilities

Explain the legal issues involved. State the law, apply it to the problem or proposed transaction and analyse the possible solutions.

5. Proposal

Propose the solution most beneficial to your client or having the strongest possibility of success and, where appropriate, seek further instructions.

6. Practical steps

Propose your recommendations for action. Who is to do what and by when? You should also establish the next point of contact (letter, telephone call or meeting) and who should initiate it.

2.4 FORM, STYLE AND LAYOUT CONVENTIONS

2.4.1 Accepted form differs

Different firms have different approaches to the art of writing letters and many firms have developed their own conventions even if they have not established a formal 'house style'. In the absence of house style, accepted practice may differ from department to department or even from fee earner to fee earner within the same firm.

For example, lawyers in the company and commercial department may write letters less formally than those in other departments, addressing a client as 'Dear Mr' rather than 'Dear Sir' from the outset of the transaction and by first name once a familiar working relationship has been established.

You may also find that a firm, a department or a particular fee-earner adopts unexpected idiosyncratic conventions. Sometimes these are 'client-driven' and you should observe them to the letter however odd they may seem. At least one City of London firm acquiesces to the slightly eccentric demands of one of the major accountancy firms, namely that no matter how senior the lawyer or how well the lawyer and accountant dealing with the matter know each other, all correspondence should be addressed to the relevant partner and the salutation should always be 'Dear Mr ...' and never 'Dear Bob' or 'Dear Tony'. This preference is based on the belief that correspondence with the firm's legal advisers looks more professional and more objective if this degree of formality is maintained.

Whilst you should follow your firm's house style if it has one, it is possible to state some basic rules and to introduce you to some common conventions.

2.4.2 Familiarity

In general, whether a client should be addressed as a personal friend is a matter of careful judgment in each case. The enforced formality in the example given above would be inappropriate if adopted for all correspondence. Nevertheless, overfamiliarity in a professional letter, even when acting for a personal friend, may diminish the sense of assurance a client is entitled to feel when receiving advice and the professional objectivity and detachment third parties would normally expect.

2.4.3 Finding an acceptable style

Writing letters to clients and others is particularly difficult for trainees. In most firms, trainee solicitors are rarely permitted to write letters in their own names. When you write to a client you will be doing so either on behalf of the firm or on behalf of someone else in the firm, often a partner. For this reason you will need to become something of a chameleon, adapting your style to accord with the preferences of your principal and of others supervising your work. You will also need to acquire the skill of 'ghosting' (see below).

Generally, your principal will expect you to use your own initiative and common sense. If you are writing on behalf of someone else, study and adopt that person's style. You should be able to find examples, both as to style generally and as to the most appropriate approach for a particular client, in the relevant files. You may also find it helpful to consult the relevant fee-earner's secretary. For example, it may be appropriate to write 'Dear Sir ' or 'Dear Madam' and end 'Yours faithfully'; or 'Dear Sir James' ending 'Yours sincerely'; or even 'Dear Jimmy' ending 'As ever'. Providing that you do not revert to your principal on every question of general style, he or she should have no objection to helping you on particularly sensitive matters.

2.4.4 'Ghosting'

In some cases, even though you may have the day-to-day conduct of the file, your principal may wish you to write as if he or she is dealing with the case personally. At first this may seem unfair to you and a deception on the client. However, it is the generally accepted practice and most clients understand that, whilst the choice of firm may be based on the reputation of a particular solicitor or the partnership as a whole, not every task will be carried out by a partner in person. It is usually sufficient that he or she has overall supervision of the matter. Nevertheless, the client will usually prefer to correspond with the partner rather than with you (be patient: your time will come).

Where a letter is written in the name of another lawyer you will need to write in his or her style and express everything as if that lawyer is dealing with the matter. However, practical difficulties can arise when 'ghosting' for another lawyer. For example, where you ask a client for further information. In such a case you may wish to avoid the potential embarrassment of a direct response to your unsuspecting principal, by drawing the relevant section of your letter to your principal's particular attention at the time it is presented for signature. On the occasions when you expect to sign the letter on your principal's behalf, indicate in the letter that the client should contact or send the information to you, the trainee. For example:

> Please contact my trainee, Hugh Jerror, who is compiling the relevant documents in this case.

You are then much less likely to find that your principal has either been wrong-footed by an unexpected telephone call or, perhaps more importantly, been sitting on the information you need in his or her in-tray.

2.4.5   Correct name, address, reference and date

Tell your secretary, before you begin to dictate the substance of the letter:

(a)   if a letter is to be marked 'by hand', 'by facsimile', 'strictly private and confidential', 'subject to contract' or 'without prejudice';

(b)   the name of the addressee, full address and salutation (if the practice at your firm is to place the address of the addressee at the end of a letter, your secretary may wish to be given the address after the body of the letter);

(c)   the addressee's reference number, if there is one, your firm's reference (usually incorporating the relevant partner's reference number and your own).

2.4.6   Correct salutation

The salutation used in a letter addressed to an individual will depend on how familiar you are with the addressee and the intended formality of the letter. For example, if you address your letter to 'The Chief Executive, Handsome plc', the salutation should be, 'Dear Sir' or 'Dear Madam' as appropriate. If your letter is addressed to a named individual, you may choose between 'Dear Sir/Madam' and, for example, 'Dear Mr Gold/Mrs Smith', 'Dear Sir James', 'Dear Jimmy', but note that your choice will determine your 'complimentary close' or ending (see below).

When writing to a business organisation or institution, letters begin, 'Dear Sirs' and end 'Yours faithfully'. When writing to a professional partnership it is traditional, but now a fairly rare practice, to use the address 'Messrs', as for example in 'Messrs Dobbs & Co.', and the salutation 'Gentlemen'.

2.4.7   'I' or 'We'

Decide whether you are writing in the name of another lawyer, in your name or in the name of the firm and be consistent. If you write a letter in the name of the firm, use the first person singular for a sole practitioner and first person plural for a partnership. In particular, avoid mixing 'I' and 'we' unless the context requires you to make the distinction. For example, you might write:

Dear Mr Gecko,

Establishment of UK subsidiary

Thank you for your letter of 17 January 1994. In answer to your enquiry, it is the firm's policy not to allow its address to be used for the purpose of providing a registered office for client companies and we are therefore unable to agree to your request. However, I have asked our company secretarial department to discuss the available options with you and, on your instructions, to make the appropriate arrangements.

Yours sincerely

2.4.8   Heading

Use headings and, where appropriate, subheadings to help your reader. Headings (and subheadings) also provide useful guidance to the person who files copies.

It is traditional to use 're' (with regard to) in headings but it is by no means obligatory. Many solicitors in modern practice regard it as entirely redundant and omit it. Another convention is to place the client's name first in the heading. So, in the case of *Hart* v *Devlin*, if you were acting for the plaintiff, your heading might be:

Re Hart v *Devlin*

Alternatively, if you were acting for the defendant, the heading, using the abbreviation 'ATS' (standing for 'at the suit of'), would read:

Devlin ATS *Hart*

In a transaction such as the sale of land, where you are acting for the vendor, the heading might be:

Re K. Illing from H. Jerror: Lame Duck House, Budgie Wharf

When acting for the purchaser:

Re H. Jerror from K. Illing: Lame Duck House, Budgie Wharf

2.4.9   Numbering

In a long letter, consider using subheadings and numbered paragraphs. Another valuable way to use numbering is where your letter seeks detailed information from your correspondent. Set it out in the form of a numbered list. This will make it easier for your correspondent to respond, and for you to check the response against the original letter.

2.4.10   Opening

If it is your first letter to the addressee explain your involvement. Otherwise acknowledge the addressee's last communication giving the date, title or other appropriate reference.

2.4.11   Ending the letter: the 'complimentary close'

The close of a letter should agree in style with the salutation. A letter beginning, 'Dear Sir' should close, 'Yours truly' or 'Yours faithfully'. When you begin a letter by a salutation which includes the addressee's surname or given name, the close should be 'Yours sincerely'. The subscription, 'Kind regards', formerly used in combination with 'Yours sincerely' to signify affection, is used increasingly in isolation as a complimentary close in itself, particularly in facsimile transmissions.

Remember to be consistent. If you have written the letter in the name of your firm, *sign* it in the firm's name, in which case it is generally thought unnecessary to type the name of the firm underneath the signature. If you have written the letter in your own name, or that of another lawyer, using the first person singular, the relevant name should be typed beneath the signature which should correspond with that name.

If you need to sign a letter written in the name of another, you can do so by placing the initials 'p.p.' or 'per pro' (abbreviations of *per procurationem*') immediately before your signature. Contrary to popular belief, the expression does not mean 'for and behalf of' but 'through the agency of'. Therefore, if you propose to sign a letter on behalf of another, you should *not* sign it:

[your signature]

pp [absent partner]

but either

> [absent partner]

> pp [your signature]

or

> pp [your signature]

> [absent partner]

Alternatively, if you prefer English to Latin you can write your signature followed by the typed words:

> Signed for [name of absent partner].

2.4.12   Final matters

Remember to specify all enclosures. The usual method is to include the word 'Enclosure' or the abbreviation 'Encl.' at the bottom left-hand corner followed by a list of enclosures.

Similarly, you should list the names of any persons to whom you intend to send copies, either by saying 'Copies to ...' or by using the abbreviation 'c.c.' (which originally stood for 'carbon copy').

2.5   SHORT, SIMPLE AND FAMILIAR WORDS

In all correspondence you should use terms that will be familiar to your reader. This means that, whilst technical terms such as 'reversionary interest', 'payment into court', 'the statutory charge' and 'joint tenant' may be permissible in letters to other lawyers, they should generally be avoided, or explained in full, when writing to a non-lawyer client or third party.

Sometimes, in a letter to a client, it is necessary to use a technical expression in the interests of precision. In such a case, without being condescending and keeping it as short and as simple as possible, you should explain what that term means. Having done so, if your explanation is a good one, you may find on re-reading your letter that you can delete the technical term after all.

Similarly, you should try to avoid jargon and 'commercialese' when writing to the lay person. Your correspondence with your client or other non-lawyer must be on a level different from that used when communicating with other lawyers or experts.

On the right occasion legal and business jargon can be useful between experts as convenient shorthand. However, you should never use jargon unless you know what it means and you know your reader knows what it means.

2.6 TONE, POLITENESS AND HUMANITY

2.6.1 Tone

When replying to correspondence the tone of the original letter or note will provide a guide to the most appropriate tone. In any event, if you take the time to clarify your aims and assess your likely readership at the preparation stage you will form a view of the particular 'tone' needed or desirable to achieve your aims and communicate your message. For example, if your correspondent is troubled, be sympathetic; if he is muddled, be particularly lucid and helpful; if he is stubborn or slow to understand, be patient without being patronising.

2.6.2 Politeness and respect

You should treat clients and others with politeness and respect but this does not mean that you have to grovel. Nor does it mean that an aggressive tone is always inappropriate. Sometimes you will need to be very firm, sometimes very conciliatory. Business people and others used to dealing with solicitors may prefer you to adopt a 'plain-speaking' style. The lay person, on the other hand, for whom a solicitor's letter is not the norm, may be intimidated by a direct or blunt tone. When dealing with company and commercial transactions you may find the tone generally used within the profession to be relatively informal and friendly when compared with the formality commonly found in correspondence between property lawyers or the aggressive writing style of many litigators. Yet these observations (even if you accept them) are only generalisations that merely serve to show that a particular tone may be entirely apt in one case and totally unsuitable in another. You must use your judgment in each case to assess your likely readership and choose an appropriate tone for the occasion.

2.6.3   Retain your composure on paper

Try not to lose your temper but, if you do, always retain your composure on paper. Never be rude or sarcastic. Rudeness reflects badly on your firm as well as on you as an individual. When you are annoyed or upset by something a client or another solicitor has said or written, pause before replying and allow yourself to cool off. When dictating, it may make you feel a lot better to let off steam and a stream of vitriol may seem deeply satisfying and even sound very impressive to you at the time. But if you send it you may live to regret it.

If there is time, put your draft letter to one side and 'sleep on it'. Once you have written your reply, read it as though you were the person receiving it. An ill-considered letter, written in anger, can sound idiotic when read in open court by counsel for the other side who will choose his or her own emphasis for the occasion.

Often the best tone to adopt when responding to another's rudeness or provocative manner is one of calm and fastidious politeness. In most cases this will show your correspondent's behaviour in its true foolish unprofessional light. Your letter will appear faultless but will have a greater retaliatory force than an ill-tempered response.

2.6.4   Humanity

Lawyers' writing is often criticised for its detachment and its failure to recognise human involvement in the legal process. Be prepared to bring people, including yourself and your firm, into your writing and your letters will seem less remote and more accessible.

The tradition in a formal letter is to use 'we' throughout when writing in the name of a partnership. Somewhat illogically, this practice is also widely adopted by single solicitors practising under a firm name. Even with a partnership the practice is archaic and anomalous. A literal reading would suggest that all the partners in the firm have joined to write the letter as a team effort. It also creates a remote and impersonal tone with the only pointer towards an individual being the reference number.

A more modern approach is to identify yourself as the author, signing the letter in your own name and using 'I' when referring to yourself and 'we' when referring to your firm. Your firm's headed notepaper will leave the reader in no doubt about the name of the firm, who 'we' refers to and your status as the author of the letter.

People are generally accustomed to being addressed in their own name or in the second person as 'you'. Most people will read the third person as referring to someone other than themselves. For example, the reader of the following letter may struggle to grasp that 'the petitioner' refers to him.

Dear Mr Hurt,

<u>Your Divorce</u>

To enforce the order it is necessary for the petitioner to swear an affidavit verifying the amount due under the order and showing how that amount has been calculated. The draft enclosed herewith should be checked against receipts and payments so that an engrossment can be prepared for swearing.

In addition to the deletion of the archaic 'herewith', the letter would benefit from active verbs which would make it clear that it is the reader who should check the contents of the draft affidavit.

2.7   LETTERS TO CLIENTS

2.7.1   Advice to clients

If you follow the suggestion in 2.3.2 you will structure your letter of advice according to the 'six Ps'. It is convenient to make the following points under the same headings.

2.7.1.1 Purpose

You should state the precise purpose for which the advice is given, making clear any limitations that apply to it. For example, if the case has an international element and the opinion is intended to be limited to English law, say so expressly.

2.7.1.2 Problem

You should set out your understanding of the problem by stating the facts as accurately as your present information permits. If there are gaps in your instructions and you need to make assumptions, say so expressly. For example,

> I am assuming for the purposes of this letter that . . . please let me know if any of these assumptions are incorrect.

If your client knows of additional facts or otherwise has a different understanding, your letter should draw this out.

2.7.1.3 Précis your conclusions

Except in the case of very short letters, it is good practice to précis or summarise your conclusions towards the beginning of a letter. This will aid your client's understanding because he or she will then be able to read the body of your letter with some knowledge of the direction your reasoning will lead.

2.7.1.4 Possibilities

The solicitors' profession is a service business whose job it is to help clients to solve problems and achieve their objectives. Clients do not exist as a privileged class whose duty is to provide you with interesting work.

Clients' interest in the law itself is usually purely transitory and they will not thank you for lengthy essays on legal niceties. Keep your explanation of the law short and simple. Exclude all references to textbooks and law reports and avoid detailed reasoning, unless you feel it to be absolutely necessary to assist the client's understanding or refute a contrary argument. An exception to this is when you are dealing with an in-house lawyer, who may want the background law in some detail.

Advice must not only be legally correct it must also be useful. A client is unlikely to regard advice that merely states the law as useful. A client usually wants an answer to a problem, and ideally wants a simple yes or no. Of course, this is rarely possible but you must explain the law in a practical way. Use analogies or examples the client is likely to understand, apply the law to the problem and, from your analysis, suggest the possible solutions. You will often need to set out a number of possibilities stating their relative advantages and disadvantages. Where the client cannot have the solution originally contemplated try to approach the problem creatively, identifying some other legally viable means of achieving the client's objective.

2.7.1.5 *Proposal*
Having set out the range of possibilities make sure that you select one as your proposal making it clear why, in your opinion, it is the solution most beneficial to your client.

Sometimes your answer will not be what the client wants to hear. It is never easy to be the bearer of bad news. If you must tell the client that he cannot have what he wants, you should give some thought to how your client will feel and exercise tact.

Having made your proposal you should seek further instructions before taking any action. The right relationship with a client is to regard it as a joint effort. You get the law right and suggest the best course of action: the client puts your work in context and makes the final decisions. Never overstep this boundary by seeking to impose a decision on a client or take it upon yourself to make the decision.

2.7.1.6 *Practical steps*
It is good practice to conclude a letter by giving an indication of the steps to be taken and who should take them. If you require further instructions from a client before you can take such a step, for example, negotiate with other solicitors, you should make this clear.

2.7.2 First instruction

Rule 15(2) of the Solicitors' Practice Rules 1990 requires solicitors to ensure, unless it is inappropriate in the circumstances, that a client knows:

(a) the name and status of the person responsible for the day-to-day conduct of a matter,

(b)   the principal responsible for its overall supervision, and

(c)   whom to approach in the event of any problems with the services provided.

The rule further requires that clients are provided, at all relevant times, with appropriate information about the issues raised and the progress of the matter.

The Law Society's Written Standards require a solicitor, at the outset of a case, to give the best information possible about the likely cost of the matter. If no fee has been agreed or estimate given, a solicitor should tell the client how the fee is to be calculated.

When confirming a client's instructions in writing a solicitor should record any agreed fee, what it covers, whether it includes VAT and disbursements and give an indication of any other reasonably foreseeable payments. If oral estimates are confirmed in writing the final amount payable may not vary substantially from the estimate unless clients have been informed of the changed circumstances in writing.

2.7.3   Keep clients informed

According to consumer surveys, the Solicitors' Complaints Bureau and the Solicitors' Indemnity Fund, the principal criticism of solicitors is that they fail to keep clients properly informed about progress. During the matter, information should be given to the client relating to its progress (or lack of progress), particularly where it may influence costs and any changes in plan for the matter.

A client will normally welcome copies of letters written to and from solicitors on the other side. You should also report to the client any significant telephone calls or meetings.

Whilst it is usually advisable to write to a third party to confirm the content of important discussions with that third party, it is not always tactful to do the same with a client. Some clients may be irritated by the perceived waste of time and paper involved, particularly when you present a bill calculated by reference to hours spent writing letters and disbursements for photocopying. However, there will be times when it is appropriate. For example, on first instruction, when your client asks you to do so, when you feel that the client would find it helpful or when you have reason to doubt the client's trustworthiness.

If in doubt, confirm it in writing.

2.7.4 Prompt response

The quality of advice you give is the most important factor both for the client and the firm. However, in most cases, it is implicit in giving your firm instructions to act that the client has faith in the firm's ability to provide practical and legally correct advice. With the possible exception of in-house lawyers, clients will assume that you are technically competent unless things go wrong. The one aspect of quality of service that a client is always able to assess is how rapidly you are dealing with the case and how promptly you respond. Always write and reply promptly. If necessary send acknowledgements or interim replies. Delays are discourteous and harm the reputation of your firm.

Never claim that you are too busy doing work for other clients. Your workload is an issue for the management of your firm and not for your client. Having taken instructions you should never ask the client to accept that the demands of another client excuse you from attending to his or her immediate needs.

If a client gives no deadline for the requested advice, do not put it to the bottom of the list and wait until you are chased. If you can write the letter of advice straight away, do so. If this is not possible, acknowledge the request but explain what has to be done, how long this is likely to take and state the date by which you propose to complete the work.

Whenever you have a deadline, try to deliver the advice *before* the date specified.

Of course, you must preserve the correct balance between delivering the client with what he or she wants when he or she wants it, and taking sufficient time to do the work carefully and completely. It will be no excuse (and no defence in negligence) to say the letter of advice was a good effort considering how little time it took to write.

Most clients will be prepared to wait, even in the most urgent of cases, if they are confident that you are not just 'sitting on it' but doing your best to provide the best solution in the shortest possible time. If the client insists on an impossible deadline, consult the partner responsible for that client for guidance on how to respond. Where necessary the partner will explain to the client that more time is needed.

2.7.5   Meetings

Although meetings can absorb alarmingly large amounts of time, they are a necessary evil. When you request a meeting with a client, confirm the time, date and place in writing. Where appropriate, enclose an agenda and indicate when you expect the meeting to end. This applies equally when writing to third parties.

2.7.6   Explain draft documents

When you send a draft document to a lay client for approval you should explain the contents of the document in a letter (or at a meeting). You should draw the attention of the client to the most salient points of the document and the importance of reading the document carefully so as to ensure that it complies with the client's requirements. You should also invite the client to query any aspect that remains unclear.

2.7.7   The voice of assurance

The need for a lawyer to be able to write with the voice of assurance is akin to the need for a medical practitioner to acquire a bedside manner. A client is entitled to feel that appropriate expertise and experience are being provided. Your choice of words and tone in correspondence should give the client no cause to doubt it. A hesitant or uncertain tone may cause the client to suspect that you do not have the expertise, even when you do.

2.7.8   Thinking and feeling

Avoid expressions such as 'I think that . . .' or 'I feel that . . .' which may suggest a lack of confidence. It is implicit that much of the content of your letter of advice amounts to your professional opinion and it is usually unnecessary to labour the point. If you feel it to be absolutely necessary, to distinguish your opinion from a statement of fact or the opinions of others, use a phrase such as, 'in my view' or 'I consider that'. An expression of this kind may also be appropriate when dealing with an unsettled or 'grey' area of law to emphasise that the view is based on a personal judgment that may prove to be incorrect. But use these words sparingly and do not allow their use to become habitual.

2.7.9 Hedging

Do not hedge or use abstract or vague expressions. One of the most commonly expressed frustrations with lawyers is that it is difficult to tie them to a definite view. Clients want clear specific advice unfettered by 'weasel words'. If the facts of a case are truly rare or the law is unclear or uncertain, say so directly. If your advice is contingent on the facts presently known, make this clear so that your client is fully aware of the risks involved.

2.7.10 Final advice

Take particular care where you have given final advice and regard the matter as complete. Unless you have made it clear that the business is concluded, you may be under a continuing obligation to a client even after the bill has been rendered and paid. You should report to the client on the outcome, explain any further action required and whether the matter will require any future review. You should also account to the client for any outstanding money and return all original documents. If the documents are to be stored by your firm or retained by way of lien, you should give details of the storage arrangements or explain the terms upon which the documents will be released.

2.8 LETTERS TO THIRD PARTIES

Whilst you will not be providing advice when writing to third parties, many of the principles mentioned in the previous section will be equally applicable. Others may apply, in varying degrees, according to the nature and purpose of the letter. There are, however, some particular points that are worth mentioning.

2.8.1 Prompt response

Clients' letters are not in a special category when it comes to the need to respond promptly. In most cases, you can only improve your client's position by responding to third parties' letters immediately, if only to acknowledge them by saying you are seeking instructions.

2.8.2   Record and confirm significant discussions

Following a significant discussion with a third party, it is usually advisable to confirm the content of that discussion in a letter to that third party.

2.8.3   Practical steps

When writing to solicitors, and others, it is good practice to state expressly how you expect the next steps to be carried out. If a step cannot be taken until a condition has been satisfied, set out the precise terms and, using the active voice, state who has responsibility for satisfying the condition.

2.8.4   'Without prejudice' letters

Without the device of 'without prejudice' correspondence, neither side to litigation could risk negotiating a compromise for fear of making potentially damaging admissions. Except in the case of a *'Calderbank* letter' (see below), a 'without prejudice' offer of compromise, cannot be used as a prejudicial admission.

However, you should exercise great care when using these words. You cannot use this expression every time you wish to say something in a letter that you may wish to deny at a later stage. The protection applies only to negotiations made in an attempt to settle a dispute. For example, if your letter is defamatory, the words will not prevent its admissibility in a libel action. Similarly, an admission in a letter headed 'without prejudice' that an individual is unable to pay debts will not be rendered inadmissible for the purposes of bankruptcy.

You will often find that solicitors include two letters in the same envelope, one 'open', the other marked 'without prejudice'. There are two main reasons for doing this. First, if the letter is not solely concerned with the settlement of a dispute, the privilege may be lost. Secondly, if the letter contains references to matters which you intend to adduce in evidence if the case proceeds to trial, it is essential that you do not include them in 'without prejudice' correspondence.

If the result of a 'without prejudice' letter is a concluded contract of compromise, the letter constitutes evidence admissible to prove the terms of the agreement.

Sometimes a letter headed 'without prejudice' contains an express provision reserving the right to refer to it in evidence solely on the issue of costs. This is known as a *Calderbank* letter. In such a case, the judge may consider the offer contained in the correspondence and make an award of costs calculated from the date upon which the party ought reasonably to have accepted the offer.

2.8.5 Subject to contract

When writing to solicitors following negotiations, for example, in a letter before exchange of contract in connection with a proposed sale of land, it is helpful to state your understanding of the deal. Despite the requirements in of the Law of Property (Miscellaneous Provisions) Act 1989, s. 2, it remains possible to create a contract for the sale of land by correspondence where the purchaser countersigns the vendor's letter and returns it along with the required deposit. It therefore continues to be common practice to mark such correspondence 'subject to contract' in the heading or in the body of the letter to avoid creating a contract by raising a presumption that the parties regard the matter as still in negotiation.

Similarly, following negotiations between parties to a proposed commercial transaction, it is usual to draw up 'heads of agreement' which record the general points of agreement. In most cases the parties contemplate the subsequent execution of a more comprehensive professionally drafted contract. Heads of agreement usually lack detail and almost always leave some matters unresolved. You should be clear about whether the heads of agreement are to bind the parties and, if so, to what extent. For example, you may intend the parties to be bound immediately by the heads of agreement but contemplate the subsequent execution by the parties of a formal contract. Although the presumption in commercial transactions is in favour of the parties intending to be bound, it is advisable to say so expressly.

Where you wish to make heads of agreement binding but also to render performance of some of the terms conditional upon the execution of the formal document, or to make only some provisions binding, such as a promise by the other party to bear your client's costs, you must say so clearly and unequivocally.

If, however, you do not intend to bind the parties at all it is advisable to use the expression 'subject to contract' or similar rather than run the risk of having to rebut the presumption in court with evidence of contrary intention.

Some firms have adopted the policy of commencing all pre-contractual correspondence with a general statement that all correspondence is intended to be subject to contract pending a formal exchange of contracts.

2.9   NOTES, MEMORANDA AND REPORTS

Most partnerships conduct internal written communications by internal notes or memoranda. The day-to-day work of your firm depends upon them. The larger your firm, the more notes and memoranda will feature in your professional life.

The two expressions are often used to mean the same thing and are then interchangeable. However, in many firms a 'note' is (in theory) a short communication concerning general administration and the internal arrangements concerning the conduct of client matters. The expression 'memorandum' is then reserved for a document intended for internal use only, which sets out the law and practice relating to a particular subject or problem. This distinction between notes and memoranda is adopted below.

2.9.1   Internal notes

In any sizeable office, notes will regularly appear on your desk. They may be addressed to everyone in the office, to those on a particular circulation list or to you personally. They will often be for information only and require no response. Where they do invite or request a reply, a simple yes or no may be appropriate and be all that is required. Others may raise a number of issues or require detail, in which case a two-page response may be justified.

Whether you are replying to an internal note or drafting an original one, if you follow the guidelines below your notes will be better received and are more likely to be read.

2.9.1.1 Layout, style and tone

Internal notes are usually laid out by first listing the addressees, and then, on separate lines, the names of any persons to whom the note is copied, the author's name, the date and the title of the subject-matter. A horizontal line, drawn across the page, then separates these details from the body of the note.

To: All Trainees

C.C: The Managing Partner and Departmental Training Partners

From: The Training Director

Date: 9 February 1994

Subject: Training Session: Legal Writing and Drafting

The session will take place on Wednesday 16 February in the training room. Coffee will be available at 9.15 a.m., prior to a 9.30 start. Please arrive promptly, bringing with you a copy of the firm's house style.

CE

Use a heading that will arrest your readers' attention. There is then no need to repeat the heading or otherwise restate what the note is about in the body of the note. Get to the point straight away.

You will probably find that there are no greater critics of your writing than your colleagues. Some of them may delight in and exploit the errors you make in internal notes. In a large firm, internal notes may be the only direct evidence of your writing seen by some of the partners who will decide your future. It makes sense not to alienate them by circulating carelessly drafted notes. Apply the same principles of good writing, and exercise the same care as you would with a letter.

Wherever possible, internal notes should be short and simple. They should be informal in tone and style, direct and free from all redundant words and expressions. Use jargon and technical words if they aid understanding or promote brevity.

Although it is not usually necessary to sign internal notes, it is common practice in many firms to include the author's initials towards the bottom left-hand corner. This is particularly apt where the author has adopted an official title in the top section as opposed to a personal name.

2.9.1.2   Avoid writing non-essential or overly long notes

Most lawyers agree that solicitors' offices are plagued by too many internal notes that are unnecessary, too long and frequently unread.

Do not develop the habit of firing off notes when a face-to-face conversation or telephone call would suffice. Many of your colleagues will regard internal notes as tiresome interruptions to their daily work. Avoid acquiring a reputation for non-essential notes, otherwise notes of genuine importance may go unread or be treated less seriously than they deserve.

When you receive a non-essential note, it may help to stem the flow of response and rejoinder to hand-write a brief endorsement on the note itself by way of reply. If the instigator of the original note sees that it did not warrant a new note in reply, he may get the message that a further exchange is unnecessary.

Some notes may set off a chain reaction causing a flurry of replies and further responses to circulate around the firm. Sometimes the nature and importance of the issue may justify a wide circulation list. You may even feel a consequent burst of further notes, both in reply to your note and to others (with luck copied to you) raising the same or related issues, to be helpful. However, in most cases, where you can foresee such a result, a note will prove a poor method of communication, unnecessarily consuming time and paper and risking confusion and frustration. A meeting is usually preferable.

The need to write notes that others may regard as unnecessary is sometimes unavoidable. It is often desirable to send a note to ensure an unequivocal and common understanding among a number of colleagues.

It is also unfortunate but true that internal notes are occasionally necessary to 'protect your back'. If you have sent a note, you can point to it at a later date and, if necessary, remind others of the exact contents.

An overlong reply is often the result of an incomplete or badly drafted note of enquiry. If you receive a note which is vague about the information required, do not be afraid to clarify the request before you draft your response. If you require information from a colleague, be clear and precise when you state your needs (and, where appropriate, state what you do *not* need). The reply is then much more likely to be short and to the point.

2.9.2 Internal memoranda

A significant part of a trainee's life is taken up with researching points of law and practice. Usually your task will be to research and write a memorandum solely for the purposes of a particular matter or client. However, if it is particularly instructive and of sufficiently wide application, you may find that (with or without some modification) your note is circulated within the practice. It may even be placed in the firm's library or the information or know-how system.

2.9.2.1 Layout
Internal memoranda follow a similar format to the internal note, usually with the addition of the words 'Internal Memorandum' at the top of the page. Use numbering systems, particularly with lengthy memoranda, but be consistent and do not abandon your numbering halfway through the note. Similarly, use subheadings where they aid understanding and cross-reference.

2.9.2.2 Style and tone
Many of the general principles applicable to letters also apply to internal memoranda but you should adopt a less formal tone. You will also have a much greater licence to use jargon and technical language but use these expressions in the interests of brevity and precision to aid communication between experts, not to impress. If such a word or expression adds nothing to the precision or economy of the document, use less esoteric language.

If the memorandum is relatively short or directed to a specific problem, structure it as you would a letter of advice:

(a)   state the purpose for which the memorandum is written;

(b)   set out the legal problem or problems to be addressed;

(c)   state the legal position and possibilities;

(d)   propose the best solutions; and

(e)   indicate any practical steps that can or should be taken.

If the memorandum is wide-ranging it may be appropriate to use the structure recommended for instructional or informative letters. This will enable each reader to grasp its main points and to select the appropriate parts to read according to his or her needs. For the same reason, for a very detailed and lengthy internal memorandum, use a structure similar to the one suggested for reports in the next section.

2.9.3   Reports

It is relatively rare for a solicitor to draft a formal report but you may be asked to do so from time to time.

A well-drafted report should be capable of being read from start to finish but also enable readers to 'skim' or 'dip-read'. Some readers will want to skim quickly through a report to obtain a general picture whilst others may wish to dip into the report to obtain a detailed view of items of particular interest.

The generally accepted format for factual reports is therefore as follows:

Title   It is important to convey the subject and scope of the report accurately in condensed form. Try to keep the title under 80 characters.

Contents page (optional)   This may also include distribution details and the keywords used by computer filing and retrieval systems.

Summary (optional)   You will often hear managers and business people referring to an 'executive summary' in a report. Where present, this can be the most important section in a report because it is the most widely read. It should summarise the subject, the conclusions and how they were arrived at in a maximum of 200 to 300 words or one page. If you include a summary, it must be capable of standing by itself.

Introduction In the introduction you should provide the background information necessary for your readers to understand the report, your terms of reference and the purpose of the report. It is usually necessary to define your terms of reference expressly. The equivalent of identifying and stating your aims, defining your terms of reference before you commence writing will save time later. You may need to clarify your instructions before you can proceed. For most reports the introduction should not be more than 400 to 500 words.

Discussion This is the main body of the report which gives an account of any investigation, events or speech witnessed, or property examined or work carried out, and the reasoning you have applied. This part will commonly be subdivided using subheadings for each section and numbering or lettering for sections, paragraphs, and subparagraphs. Full details and supporting material may be contained in appendices.

You must decide whether you are going to give conclusions at the end of each section or withhold them until towards the end of the report grouping them under a separately headed section. The second method is used more frequently than the first. With a particularly lengthy report a combination of the two methods can be very effective.

Conclusions Taken in conjunction with the introduction this section should give the reader the gist of the report. If you have given conclusions in the relevant parts of the main body of the report, keep this section short and limit it to containing the conclusion of the main points argued in the discussion.

You should arrive at your conclusions as objectively as possible. Where there are conflicting facts or opinions, you should present both sides of the argument so that the reader can verify the validity of your conclusions. However, you should introduce no new facts and opinions at this stage.

Recommendations Your recommendations, the consequential action to be taken if your conclusions are accepted, should be a distinct section. In this section you should set out the action that should be taken. Whereas the conclusions give a completely objective view of the information presented, recommendations may be subjective.

Appendices (optional)   Appendices should contain supporting material such as documents referred to, verbatim statements, technical specifications and tables of figures, results of experiments, and detailed analysis. Although this material may be highly relevant, it should be contained in appendices where it would impair the reader's rapid assimilation of the essential material were it contained in the main body of the report. On the other hand, if the reader needs this information to follow the arguments, it should not be in an appendix but in the text.

2.10   CHECKING

2.10.1   Nobody gets it right first time

Although time spent in planning and preparation usually results in far less editing, errors may still be present. You should always check a letter, note, memorandum or report thoroughly.

2.10.1.1   Initial revision and 'sleep on it'
The first step is to read your work thoroughly. Then, once you have checked it for obvious errors and ambiguities, put your writing to one side and 'sleep on it'. Leave it over night, over lunch or while you deal with your post or telephone messages. You will then return to it with a fresh mind.

2.10.1.2   The extra eye of a stranger
Better still, ask someone else to check it. Most writers develop writing habits that make it difficult to see the errors or ambiguities that may be obvious to a stranger. However, do not exhaust the goodwill of your colleagues with routine checking, reserve it for the most important occasions when the particular complexity or sensitivity requires an 'extra eye'.

2.10.1.3   Vocalise
Alternatively, try reading your work aloud. If you vocalise your writing you will highlight faults your eyes normally miss. This is particularly true

of punctuation mistakes. Of course, in most offices reading aloud is often not possible. In such a case, read slowly and 'sub-vocalise' by sounding the words in your head.

2.10.1.4   Check the whole document

The accuracy and completeness of the body of your letter will be uppermost in your mind but do not undervalue the importance of checking *every* detail. Particularly mundane aspects such as the addressee's name and address are important, not least to the addressee. A client or other reader will be unimpressed if these items are incorrect and your lack of diligence may undermine your advice or argument and the reader's estimation of the overall competence of your firm.

2.10.1.5   Check that you have properly addressed your readers' needs

With the addressee's needs in mind ask yourself, 'Have I answered those needs?' A brilliant explanation of the law is not necessarily all the client needs. Will the addressee get the message you want to convey, or will your writing be seen as a collection of interesting, well-informed legal thoughts leading nowhere in particular?

Your letter must be intelligible, not just to you but also to the addressee. Put yourself in your reader's shoes. Ask yourself, 'Will he or she understand this?' Different backgrounds, educational levels and many other factors make each situation different. Placing yourself in your reader's shoes may also help you to spot any over-long sentences or clumsy expressions.

2.10.1.6   Things to look out for

As you read your writing, mark any changes you want to make. You should not only be examining the content of what you have written but thinking about how the document reads. You will need to edit for clarity and organisation; for style, usage and tone; and for layout and presentation. Spelling and typographical errors call for particular attention.

2.10.1.7   Check the spelling

Poor spelling creates a bad impression, reflects badly on the reputation of your firm, and may cause your readers to lose faith in you and dismiss your work.

English, having many words which seemingly follow no discernible pattern, has many spelling traps. In addition, most people have spelling 'blind spots' and tend to miss particular errors when proofreading their work. Get to know your spelling weaknesses and make a special effort to look out for them when checking. Remember that responsibility for correct spelling lies with you. Do not think that you can delegate the responsibility for correct spelling to your secretary, still less rely upon the solicitor supervising your work.

2.10.1.8   Typographical errors
Even if you have followed the suggestion in 1.11.4 (to avoid using words of similar sound) it is still easy to fail to spot a rogue 'employee' when you intended to write 'employer'. So make a point of looking out for words of a similar sound such as 'employer/employee', 'mortgagor/ mortgagee', 'lessor/lessee' and double-check that the word is the one you intended.

Chapter Three

Drafting

3.1 AIMS

The first step in preparation is the identification of aims. In one sense, your aims in drafting are easily identified: as a general rule, you should give effect to your client's intentions by ensuring that your document is:

● accurate: aim to embody the client's instructions in your draft;

● complete: aim to deal with all eventualities that ought to be covered;

● precise: aim to avoid ambiguity;

● clear: aim to draft in a style that is readily comprehensible;

● contemporary: aim to use only words in modern usage and delete archaic expressions;

● short and simple: aim to 'keep it short and simple': the 'KISS' principle.

The words preceding these general aims are all-important: you should aim to give effect to your client's intentions. The most important aims are those of your client.

3.2   TAKING INSTRUCTIONS

3.2.1   Know what the client wants to achieve: understand the transaction

Before you put pen to paper (or switch on the dictating machine) you must know what it is that the client wishes to achieve. One of the worst things a lawyer can do is to rush into producing an inappropriate document for a transaction. You must first understand the transaction fully both from a legal and a personal or business point of view.

Find out the scale of the transaction. A partner in one leading firm once made the following analogy: 'Documents are like cars, they can be Rolls Royces or Minis and it is not always appropriate to drive up in a Rolls Royce'.

If the transaction has an international element make sure that you take into account any national or cultural differences involved. For example, there are different practices and different expectations in relation to documentation in America and continental Europe. You should also be careful in the words you use. For example, to an American lawyer the word 'liquidate' merely means 'turn assets into cash'.

Make an effort to get to know the client and, if the matter in hand is a business transaction, learn about the client's business and commercial objectives. Check that you are not making any false assumptions. Clients will rarely have thought of everything relevant to the transaction and they do not always mean what they say or say what they mean. Sometimes, you may need to look behind what your clients are saying to identify their real aims and needs.

When in doubt it is best to assume that the client is not aware of all the types of information you will need and the issues that need to be covered. In particular, once you have an understanding of the commercial aspects of the transaction you will need to assess and discuss the need for special terms designed to provide legal protection against identified risks [see Traps and Pitfalls, below]. Doing this at an early stage will make the client appreciate that you are providing a tailor-made document and dispel any notion that you are merely filling in the client's name on an existing all-purpose precedent.

3.2.2 Are you satisfied that you understand how the transaction will work?

Try to think yourself into the transaction. Are you satisfied that you understand how it will work? If necessary draw a diagram showing the interrelationship of parties, the route by which title to property or funds are to pass, or the various sequences of possible events.

Think about the practicalities. For example, check that the negative pledge in a loan agreement is not drafted so generally that the borrower is prevented from entering into normally acceptable arrangements such as the creation of a repairer's lien on vehicles, plant or machinery or retention of title agreements. Similarly, is the cross-default clause so general that an immaterial event such as a failure to pay the office milk bill may be treated as an event of default? Sometimes potential practical difficulties are not so obvious. In one case, a manufacturer was happy to give an undertaking to the government that the local content of his company's product would be kept above a certain level. It was only when his lawyers checked with him how in practice he would do this that he realised that, in some circumstances, compliance might be impossible and that the undertaking would have to be qualified before it was acceptable.

In a relatively new or unusual type of transaction, vision and imagination are particularly important. Without it an entire area could be completely overlooked. This need becomes acute where technology is involved. Computer contracts entered into 10–15 years ago often provide examples. A firm commissioning the design of a computer system might neglect to deal in the contract with the copyright and intellectual property rights. The consequence, discovered years later, would be that the firm had no ownership in the software and, technically, even its right to use the software might be questionable. Many pop stars of the 1960s, who receive nothing from revival footage released on video or even music re-released on CD, must lament the myopia of their lawyers' failure to anticipate such developments by drafting a clause along the lines of the now-established 'change media rights' clause.

3.2.3 Consider the most appropriate structure to achieve the client's objectives

A client may come to you with a firm view of the legal form which the intended transaction should take. Nevertheless, you should ask yourself whether the transaction structure contemplated by your client is the most appropriate one. Could the same result be achieved in a more efficient or advantageous way using a different form or structure?

No client or case is exactly the same and no fixed rule can be advanced. The extent to which you pursue potential alternatives with your client will depend upon the client's standing and experience of entering into legal transactions of this kind. Some clients have acquired a sound understanding of the law and (sometimes through years of experience of similar transactions) have a clear view of the legal relationship or result they wish to effect. They simply come to you or your firm because they wish to rely on documentation drafted with professional skill. Others may not appreciate the range of possibilities until you bring them to their attention.

You should check (with tact) that the client has sufficient grasp of the legal possibilities, options and risks and their consequences. The client's initial assumptions may be wrong. For example, does the client want to create an agency or a distributorship?

Sensibly approached most clients will appreciate your initiative but never seek to usurp the client's free choice. Ultimately it is for your client to follow your advice or not and, in particular, to make commercial decisions.

3.2.4   Other matters

3.2.4.1   What authority will the client (and other parties) need?
You should always check that all parties to a transaction will have the necessary authority. An individual signing personally may need to be full age, sound mind and acting in his or her own right. An employee must have the full authority of his or her employers. You may need to investigate the terms of the authority of a person claiming to act in a fiduciary capacity, such as agent or trustee. In the case of a company or corporation it will usually be necessary to trace the chain of authority through the memorandum and articles of association and the decisions of its board.

3.2.4.2   What are the tax implications?
It may be desirable to ask specifically whether your client requires advice on the tax implications of a matter and to confirm the instructions in

writing. You may not be a tax expert but a solicitor should have a general idea of the likely tax treatment of the transaction. How is the transaction treated for VAT? Is stamp duty payable? You should also know enough to realise when a tax specialist should be consulted.

3.2.4.3 Are other professional advisers involved?

It is advisable to identify any other professional advisers involved, and to establish their respective roles and areas of responsibility at the earliest stage. It may be appropriate to contact them to verify the position. It may also be appropriate to contact the lawyers or other professionals acting on behalf of other parties.

3.2.4.4 What is the proposed timetable and what time periods are relevant?

The proposed timetable should be established from the outset. Deadlines and critical dates or events should be noted. If you think the client's timetable unfeasible say so at an early stage but try to be as constructive as possible, explaining why you take this view and putting forward a revised timetable.

Relevant periods of time should be carefully noted. Are clear days required or can partial days be included? Are any provisions for deemed service of notice applicable? Are there any time-limits on doing anything else, e.g. the 21 day time-limit for registering charges at Companies House? Have all important time-limits been drawn to the client's attention?

3.2.4.5 When is the contractual relationship or the effect of the document to come to an end?

If the parties contemplate ending their relationship by notice, what form should that notice take and what should the time period be? If the happening of events is to bring the relationship to an end, what are they and is termination to be automatic or at one party's option? What will be the consequence of termination in any of these cases?

3.2.4.6 Default: what could go wrong and which of the parties will bear responsibility?

What is the machinery and how is it to operate if things go wrong? Who will be responsible? One of the main purposes of a contract (and many other documents) is to eliminate the possibility of misunderstanding as to what happens and who is responsible if problems occur. Clients are often reluctant in the euphoria at the eve of a contractual relationship even to contemplate the possibility that things might go wrong, and it can be difficult to persuade a client to consider what the consequences should be. It is your responsibility to make sure that these matters are addressed and that the document is not the cause of costly litigation.

3.2.4.7 Note the client's bargaining position – who will prepare documents?

It is always an advantage to put forward your own draft. Not only will the document be in your own style, but you have the opportunity to plan it according to the structure you want and incorporate the most favourable terms right from the start. This is infinitely preferable to the laborious task of trying to alter somebody else's draft. However, you should not assume that it will always be your client who puts forward the draft. In many situations the bargaining position of the other party may be such that your role is one of approving the draft of another firm. Similarly, in some transactions, it is customary for one party to prepare the draft, for example, in the case of share purchase and sale agreements it is usual for the purchaser's solicitors to draft the contract.

Where you find yourself in the position of approving another firm's draft it is often helpful to rehearse the transaction as if you were preparing the draft so that you are properly armed with an idea of your optimum when it comes to negotiating amendments.

A document prepared by another lawyer will, of course, use the style and conventions of that lawyer's firm. If the draft misses out a provision that you think the document should contain, you must press for it to be included. If the wording of the draft is confusing or ambiguous, then you should insist on alteration. But, provided the draft includes the right provisions, and they are expressed clearly, it is not appropriate for you to seek to make purely stylistic improvements. Do not try to score points: it will not impress the client but it could obstruct negotiation and add unwelcome tension, possibly leading to the breakdown of dealing.

3.2.4.8 Summarise and seek confirmation from the client: if in doubt clarify your instructions

Taking instructions is an interactive rather than a passive process. This means listening and understanding as well as writing and drafting clearly.

The cause of many negligence claims can be traced to a failure in communication. If any matter remains unclear you should *always* seek clarification. Make a careful note of the meeting or telephone call and place it on the file. Once you have a sufficient grasp of the essentials, summarise them for your client to verify. It may also be helpful, in appropriate circumstances, to send a copy of your notes to the client. Wherever possible, it is good practice to give an indication of the approach you intend to take so that you can receive confirmation (or otherwise) at the earliest of stages. Doing this can save a lot of wasted time, and possibly embarrassment, later.

3.3 ARE YOUR AIMS IN TUNE WITH THOSE OF YOUR CLIENT?

Ideally there should be a 'meeting of minds' during the instructions process. You should encourage your client to see the production of the document as a joint effort between legal adviser (other advisers) and the client. It is, therefore, vital at this stage that you check that you are on the same wavelength as your client. Not only should you understand the client's position and objectives but you should try to ensure also that the client understands your position as a solicitor and the legal implications of the transaction. Are your respective aims in tune?

3.3.1 Completeness and precision

Your client may not wish the document to cover every eventuality or a provision to be too specific.

Your draft should deal with all eventualities which *ought* to be covered. What ought to be covered is neither exclusively a matter for you nor for your client. Ideally it should be determined by your client in the light of your advice.

You must analyse the transaction in terms of each step that must be taken by the parties and use a form of words which will bring about performance in precisely the manner required by your client. The court will not imply a missing term unless it is necessary to give the contract business efficacy, and even then it must be a term which, objectively determined, the parties would have agreed to but was too obvious to be expressly included. You must also identify the risks to which your client is exposed, and the steps that can be taken to protect against them.

However, your client may not wish the document to cover absolutely all contingencies or a provision within it to be too precise or specific. Your client may prefer performance to be within a reasonable time rather than within a stated period or, in a will, may prefer to leave a decision to be made by an executor. In many commercial negotiations a client may prefer a provision which does not go into great detail. This may be because the client wishes to leave an issue open (or ajar) by the use of an expression such as 'material' or 'reasonable' or because the risk which the suggested provision is intended to protect against is considered by the client to be negligible and outweighed by the commercial value of closing the deal.

3.3.2 Clear and contemporary

When drafting you should have at least three classes of reader in mind. First your client, who will want to understand the document if only to be satisfied that it accords with his or her instructions. Many commercial clients now realise that contracts are working documents rather than records to be put away in a drawer or filing cabinet until litigation is threatened. Such clients will not wish to revert to you on each occasion the document is referred to for an explanation of its meaning. All documents drafted by lawyers, with the possible exception of pleadings, are drafted principally for the benefit of lay clients and should be capable of being understood by them, albeit after initial explanation of technical words and concentrated reading. You should not need your client to tell you to avoid useless archaic legal expressions but you may wish to adjust the approach you take and the words you use according to your assessment of the client.

Secondly, you should consider other parties to the document. This is particularly important in documents intended to regulate consumer relationships. The language you use should be adjusted accordingly. On occasions you may find it desirable to provide definitions for lay persons which are normally unnecessary for legal precision. For example, some terms carry statutory definitions, such as 'month' (Law of Property Act 1925, s. 61), and in law a definition expressed in identical terms would be superfluous. But if it might be helpful in a document in regular use by lay persons there is no harm in including it.

Thirdly, your ultimate reader may be a judge and the need for precision is therefore acute. The use of technical expressions may provide legal precision for the benefit of the judge or other lawyer but may be unintelligible to the lay person. Even though you should aim for your document to make sense to a lay client, often words that have a specific legal meaning have to be used. An unambiguous document may not be immediately intelligible to the lay person. Achieving the right balance between unambiguity and intelligibility in a document can be very difficult. Where it is necessary for the client's protection, precision should always prevail over intelligibility. But make sure that the expressions you use are really necessary and that their meaning is explained to the client where appropriate.

3.3.3   Short and simple

Since lay people are inclined to regard unnecessary length and complexity as a feature of lawyer's work your aim to keep things short and simple is unlikely to meet with objection. Use ordinary short words and avoid legal jargon and intricacy of expression. The nearer you can get to words of one or two syllables, the clearer your work will be.

However, do not confuse your duty to use plain English with the desire to reduce the length of your document. Your efforts to be complete and precise will sometimes be received with less than a warm welcome. Often your draft will deal with contingencies which had not occurred to your client.

You may have to make special efforts in certain cases. The client may specifically ask that the document be 'short and simple'. For example, a bank lending to corporate borrowers with the highest of credit ratings may not wish you to include all the standard protection in quite the same Draconian force as might be appropriate for other borrowers. The same bank, possibly in pursuit of a plain-English initiative, may wish documentation intended for its personal customers to include protection 'up to the hilt' but expressed in terms the average customer is likely to understand.

Whilst the 'kiss' principle should always be present in your mind, beware of trying to oversimplify the documentation to please the client. If the substance of a transaction is complex, the risk to which your client is exposed is high or the law highly technical, there is no getting away from your duty to ensure that your client understands the position and to draft the document accordingly.

3.4   THE CONTENTS AND PRINCIPAL CLAUSES

Perhaps the most obvious step in preparing a document is to identify the provisions it ought to contain. However, it is surprising how often lawyers overlook vital considerations at this stage in their enthusiasm to get on with the drafting.

The provisions a draft ought to contain fall into the following categories:

(a)   terms required by statute (or made necessary by statutory intervention);

(b)   terms required at common law;

(c)   terms made necessary by external documents;

(d)   terms fundamental to the operation of the transaction; and

(e)   standard protective terms.

3.4.1   Terms required by statute (or made necessary by statutory intervention)

The statutory provisions relevant to your document will naturally vary from one field of law to another, but you need to be sure that you have identified anything that may affect the validity or applicability of your document.

In many areas, requirements are laid down by statute. The Consumer Credit Act 1974, for example, lays down detailed requirements for agreements, notices and advertisements. You need to look out for the occasions when an Act automatically incorporates a term into a document unless it is expressly excluded. For example, in articles of association under the Companies Act or terms as to description or quality in contracts for the supply of goods or services. Where you do not want such a term to be implied, you must remember to exclude it expressly, taking care to ensure that the clause will remain valid under the Unfair Contract Terms Act 1977.

The Unfair Contract Terms Act 1977 is of wider application than is sometimes realised. In commercial transactions, be particularly careful where the document you are drafting might be brought within the Act as being the 'standard terms' upon which your client deals. Another potentially hazardous area of very general application is European competition law (arts 85 and 86 of the Treaty of Rome).

Sometimes an Act or other provision may have the effect of requiring a further step to be undertaken if a particular term is included, for example, the Companies Act 1985 requires registration of documents that create charges and the Restrictive Trade Practices Act 1976 requires registration of certain restrictive agreements.

Another crucial area of concern is insolvency legislation. Make sure that you have a sufficient knowledge of the effect on transactions of the appointment of an administrator, an administrative receiver, a receiver and a liquidator and the differences between them. In the case of an individual, what would be the effect of bankruptcy? You will be severely handicapped if you do not have an understanding of insolvency law because you will not be in a position to work out where your client will stand should these events occur to other parties.

3.4.2 Terms required at common law

Common law requirements are generally better known and on the whole much less onerous than statutory requirements. Nevertheless it is surprising how often lawyers, particularly specialists, become so entranced with particular statutory or other requirements that they seem to forget the most basic principles, for example, that a guarantee requires consideration if it is not contained in a deed, or that past consideration will not support a promise as a binding contractual obligation.

Again, a knowledge of the effects of insolvency is important as is the availability of equitable remedies. If the other party becomes insolvent will your client be left with nothing but an unsecured claim? Will this be good enough? Would specific performance of your contract be available to save your client in these circumstances?

Make sure that you are clear on the differences at common law between terms, representations and indemnities.

Keep in mind the possibility of things going wrong. When will a party be in default and what would the consequences be?

Remember the distinction between conditions and warranties. Although the expression 'warranty' (used in its technical sense to mean a term of a secondary nature the breach of which gives rise to damages only) is falling out of judicial favour (see *Moschi* v *Lep Air Services Ltd* [1973] AC 331) and the idea of the intermediate 'innominate' term is becoming more popular, there is still no doubt that only the breach of a condition (a term going to the root of the contract) will automatically give the right to terminate. It is no good simply to state that the term is a 'condition' (see *L. Schuler AG* v *Wickman Machine Tool Sales Ltd* [1974] AC 235). If it is important for your client to be able to repudiate the contract upon breach without fear of an argument that the term broken was a mere warranty rendering the repudiation wrongful, it is best to provide expressly for a right to terminate in addition to any right to damages or other remedy.

If your client wishes to make provision for liquidated damages, make sure that you know the principles surrounding penalty clauses and the difference between a liquidated damages clause which operates on breach (and which is capable of attack under the penalties doctrine) and a clause which merely operates on termination (and is unaffected by the penalties doctrine). The reason why clauses apparently requiring more than actual loss survive the penalties doctrine is that they have been drafted so as to operate on the happening of a specified event, which is not an event of default but gives a party a right to terminate. If the parties have further agreed that, in such an event, a sum becomes payable, the courts are merely asked to enforce the agreement. There is no question of liquidated damages because there is no breach. There can therefore be no offence to the rule against penalties. For example, a prepayment clause in a loan agreement which allows a borrower to prepay can provide for a sum to become payable in addition to interest and the return of capital. This sum does not have to be calculated by reference to a formula which attempts to pre-estimate loss because there is no breach on prepayment.

3.4.3 Is your document affected by other documents (and might other documents be affected by your document)?

The terms of agreements and documents frequently impose requirements on the form of documents executed under them. A charge may set out the circumstances in which a receiver can be appointed, the form of that appointment and the manner of its execution. A debenture stock trust deed may have precise requirements as to the certificates that have to be given before there can be a further issue. A lease may contain formal time and other requirements in relation to rent reviews. If your document is affected by another document, it is important to identify exactly what the requirements are. If the precedent you are planning to use (or another firm's draft) imposes strict formal requirements which might be overlooked by your client when the time comes, redraft the clause so that there are no critical steps to be taken.

3.4.4 Terms fundamental to the operation of the transaction

It is difficult to overlook a fundamental term, but not beyond lawyers to do so. Before you get weighed down with detail it is helpful at the planning stage to pause, and ask, 'What are the essential things that this document must do?' Before you do anything else take the time to ensure that the key clauses do what they should do. Once you have identified the terms fundamental to the operation of the transaction you should consider how they may be tailored and supplemented so as to achieve exactly what the client wants.

This is where the extra effort you made in taking instructions pays off. For example, if in a private company acquisition it transpires that your client wishes to buy the target company not so much for its brand names, its distribution network or its profitability but in order to acquire its research team, then this should influence the way you draft the share purchase agreement. In such a case you might draft the agreement so as to require detailed 'golden handcuff' service contracts to be entered into by members of the research team as a condition of completion.

3.4.5 Standard protective terms: boilerplate

One of the skills you must acquire is the ability to analyse a transaction and be able to imagine all the things that could go wrong. You will then be in a position to anticipate problems by ensuring that your client is properly protected. You will usually find standard protective terms in precedents. These terms are often referred to as 'boilerplate'. The expression probably derives from the identification plates attached to boilers during their manufacture which contain standard information as to the capacity of the boiler, the pressure it can contain, and so on. The plate contains blank boxes so that the appropriate information can be stamped on to the plate. Another theory holds that in the USA in the 19th century, local newspapers reprinted syndicated material provided to them in the form of ready-to-use printing plates: putting together a newspaper was just a matter of assembling the plates on a cylinder printing press rather like assembling a boiler with copper plate.

Boilerplate terms are terms which do not have to be included in a document for it to be valid and effective but are normally included for the protection of one or other party. For example, an entire agreement clause; a *force majeure* clause; a further assurance clause; a confidentiality clause; a governing law clause; a submission to the jurisdiction clause; a 'time of the essence' clause; a costs clause; a notices clause; a restriction on announcements clause; an anti-waiver clause; a foreign currency indemnity; a tax grossing-up clause; an assignments clause; and a disputes determination clause. A solicitor who failed without good reason to include such terms in an appropriate case could be exposed to a negligence claim.

Many of the larger firms have developed standard boilerplate terms to be incorporated (after appropriate modification) to all agreements. If you have a set of standard boilerplate terms to hand or you are using a precedent containing such terms, read the boilerplate very carefully and do not assume that every clause or even any clause in its existing form will be appropriate. You will always need some protective provisions; you never need all.

In the absence of a set of standard boilerplate terms you can normally identify the appropriate terms by looking at reliable precedents. It is best to look at more than one precedent (and preferably from different sources) to guard against mistakes or terms omitted for special reasons. Draw up a list of the terms you think you will need at the start of the planning process and tick them off as you draft the document.

3.5 TRAPS AND PITFALLS CHECKLIST

Tax	What are the tax implications of the transaction?
Registers	Are there any registers which should be searched or in which the transaction should be recorded ?
Authority	Have all parties to the transaction the necessary authority?
Periods	Have you carefully noted all relevant time periods?
Standard terms	Does the document contain all the usual standard protective terms or 'boilerplate'?
Practicalities	Have you thought about how the transaction will work and any practical difficulties there may be?
Insolvency	What would happen if a party became insolvent?
Termination	In what circumstances will the effect of the document come to an end?
Failures	What is the machinery and how is it to operate if things go wrong?
Attendance note	Have you recorded in an attendance note and placed on file for further reference (and for your protection) any important item of information communicated orally?
Liquidated damages, penalties and termination payments	Do you wish to provide for pre-estimated losses and, if so, are they to be payable as a result of breach or following exercise of a specific right to terminate?
Limitation and exclusion clauses	Exercise extra care to ensure that these clauses are unambiguous and that they are not likely to be rendered invalid by the Unfair Contract Terms Act 1977 or other statutory or common law rules.
Specific performance	Are you confident that you know the principles and the circumstances in which specific performance would be available in your transaction? This may be crucial in cases of default or insolvency.

3.6   PLANNING BEFORE DRAFTING

Always prepare a plan of the document as a logical structure. Having gained a sound understanding of the transaction, perhaps having drawn up a diagram, and identified the terms the particular document should contain, you should group them under broad headings which should be set out in logical and natural order. Start with major headings and once you have the essential structure for your document, expand the headings into clauses and subclauses.

If you follow this procedure, provisions relating to a particular topic will be properly grouped together and not scattered at random throughout the document. Further, this process will not only provide you with a structure to work with but may also help to indicate gaps of which you were previously unaware.

Definitions are among the most difficult provisions to draft and benefit from careful planning. Allocate a separate sheet for a plan of the words and expressions you will need to define and draft provisional definitions. Keep the list to hand as you develop your plan and as you draft the document. As you proceed you may find that you need to add a new definition or amend an earlier one. Make a note each time a definition is required in a clause and review the definition in the context of the provision in which it occurs. If you do this you will minimise the chance of incorporating a flawed definition in your draft and when you come to draft the interpretation clause (often the most lengthy), you will find that, but for some fine-tuning and sorting into alphabetical order, you have already drafted the clause.

Most documents should tell a story and their natural order is therefore a chronological succession of performance, events and actions. In an agreement, first the commencement provision will set out the parties, then the recitals (if any) may describe the parties' background and what they want to do. Next will come the definitions followed by the operative provisions which are usually best laid out to describe what the parties are going to do and when, what will happen if they fail, when the relationship will end and what happens then.

For example a contract of employment will usually broadly conform to the following order:

Appointment
Period of employment
Duties
Remuneration
Holidays
Sickness
Termination

3.7 PRECEDENTS

3.7.1 How to use precedents

All lawyers use precedents – modern legal practice relies on them. It is simply not feasible or cost-effective for a solicitor to draft documents such as a company's articles of association or a bank mortgage from scratch. With most transactions failure to consult a precedent book or other similar source would be a waste of accumulated know-how and valuable time. A good precedent may embody decades of experience, follow a statutory or generally recognised form and indicate the provisions which are generally found in such transactions.

With most transactions you will usually be able to find a useful precedent, whether in an encyclopaedia of forms and precedents or in the file of an earlier case. Many solicitors' firms now have precedent banks linked to their word processing systems. Indeed, the word processor has become invaluable in the production of documents which have standard clauses. There is no need to write or dictate a standard clause if it is held in a template in the system. The computerised precedent bank, like the written precedent, is a very useful tool which, if used properly, can save valuable time and effort for the solicitor and solicitor's fees for the client.

However, precedents and precedent banks can have their disadvantages. Precedents should not be allowed to become a substitute for thought or analysis. Unfortunately, many lawyers attempt to skip the planning stage and go straight to a precedent. They then seek to graft on further provisions required for the particular transaction. This approach is bad for a number of reasons.

The form of a document should, primarily, be determined by your client's instructions and not by the product of an earlier transaction which has no or little connection with your client or your thinking. Precedents are the result of particular considerations which will almost certainly be different in some respects from those pertaining to your client's transaction. It is therefore unsafe to 'tinker' with a document designed and negotiated for another transaction, instead of beginning with your own design.

A further criticism of this approach is that lawyers who adopt it tend only to add to the document. In addition to increasing the length of the document, by failing to delete unnecessary or irrelevant material, there will have been little or no critical analysis of the clauses drawn from the precedent and old bad habits may be perpetuated. The ease with which modern computer technology can be used to produce documents based on precedents has arguably done the profession almost as much harm as it has good. For evidence that precedents on word processors have become the 'lazy lawyer's charter', you will not have to look far. For example, many leases contain clauses dealing with all kinds of events which, given the nature of the tenancy in question, are at best improbable and often quite impossible.

You are not 'drafting' if you copy out the first precedent you find, simply adding parties, dates and the like. This is mere form-filling.

Precedents are, or should be, no more than valuable reminders of the provisions commonly found in a transaction of a particular type. They provide a checklist to help you decide on the terms you need for a particular transaction and remind you to guard against known traps and pitfalls. It is dangerous to assume that precedents can be used in precisely the form in which they appear. They do not provide exhaustive answers.

The correct approach is first to plan your document and next to prepare a rough first draft. Only then should you refer to your precedent, using it as if you were obtaining a second opinion. It may be reassuring to find that the precedent is similar to your own draft. This probably means that you can be reasonably confident that you are on the right track.

Never think that a precedent cannot be improved, and always be suspicious if, at first sight, it appears that no changes are called for. If the precedent has a clause not present in your draft do not add it automatically. Examine its purpose carefully and, if you think it appropriate to incorporate a clause of this type, consider whether you can improve upon the way it has been drafted.

Here are some guidelines:

Find the best and most up-to-date precedents Always refer to more than one precedent. Do not use the first precedent that comes to hand. Make sure that you have selected the best and most up-to-date precedents available. Always consider the background and 'pedigree' of a precedent. Who drafted it, how experienced was the draftsman and who, and what transaction, was it drafted for?

Make the precedent fit your own transaction Never adopt a precedent without change. A precedent can always be improved: make it your own by adapting it for your transaction. It is often best to write out each clause by hand, rephrasing it as you go along.

Delete unnecessary or redundant language Do not allow a precedent to lead you back into bad habits. Delete archaic and other redundant words. If necessary redraft the clause in plain English.

Understand the legal principles underlying each passage Make sure that you understand the function and purpose of each clause. Never include a provision merely because it is contained in a precedent. It may have been included to deal with very particular circumstances not present in your case or transaction. On the other hand, it may need to be included for good reason. So find out what the purpose of the clause is and only then decide to incorporate or discard it.

Test the necessity of every provision in the precedent: what is it there to guard against? Ask yourself whether this term is really necessary. Has it ever been relied on? Do not persist with irrelevant or obsolete provisions just because they have always been included. Is it designed to protect against a minor contingency that is very unlikely to occur?

Test the necessity for provisions in your draft not present in the precedent Similarly, if you have extra provisions in your draft which do not appear in your precedent, ask yourself whether they are really necessary. Are you being verbose? What are your reasons for including the provision? Remember to test each provision against the needs of your client.

Keep the client's aims in mind Keep in mind the client's objective and your reason for selecting this particular legal form of transaction. It may be that the person who drafted the document upon which the precedent is based did so under very different circumstances. For example, the transaction may have been driven by tax considerations prevailing and relevant to the particular client at that time. Having identified your client's precise needs do not add back unnecessary provisions simply because they are in the precedent.

3.7.2   Build your own precedent bank

Most practitioners build their own precedent files containing precedents of completed transactions. Whilst it would be absurd to keep a spare copy of everything, if you preserve, in a dedicated precedent file, copies of documents for which there was no suitable precedent at the time or examples of variants on a theme, you may find that your effort will be rewarded in the future. If your firm does not have a centralised precedent bank, find out which of your colleagues keeps precedent files and in which areas.

3.7.3   Standard forms

Some firms have developed standard forms for particular types of transaction. They differ from precedents (which are the by-product of a particular transaction reflecting a negotiated deal). Standard forms are documents *created* for future use, often complete with optional variations which you select according to the circumstances, together with detailed guidance notes. They will usually be tailored to the advantage of a particular type of client, e.g. the lender in a loan agreement.

Whilst many of the comments made concerning precedents are also applicable, in varying degrees, to standard forms, if your firm has invested the research resources necessary to produce them the partners will not expect you to deviate from the form without good reason. But remember: no transaction is exactly like another and no document is beyond improvement.

3.8   LAYOUT CONVENTIONS AND HOUSE STYLE

3.8.1   Consistency of layout

Consistency of layout is just as important as consistency in the use of words. A well-drafted document should be easy to read, and consistent layout of the text can be a significant aid to easy reading. Bad or inconsistent layout can be seriously misleading. If you begin to list items one to a line, you should not later deviate arbitrarily by including two in one line. If you indent each subclause from the margin and then further indent paragraphs within subclauses, any later paragraphs indented only once may be misread as subclauses. At the very least, inconsistency of layout creates a bad impression.

Despite the words of Lord Sumner in *Yorkshire Insurance Co. Ltd* v *Campbell* [1917] AC 218 that 'founts of type have no legal meaning' (10 differing founts had been used), it is thought that today a court may well take a different view. It is therefore unsafe and unwise to allow inconsistency of layout to creep into your drafting.

3.8.2   Long paragraphs and sentences

Traditionally provisions of Acts of Parliament and private documents were set out in long continuous sentences, often of up to 20 lines (sometimes more), each line extending from margin to margin. Often, the whole of a document would be constructed grammatically as a single continuous sentence with only an occasional capital initial or word underlined. The original reason for this may have been (the earliest of documents being hand-written on parchment a single line of which might be as long as two feet) the draftsmen wished to save parchment. Another possible explanation is that it was done so as to leave no space for fraudulent addition.

However, around 100 years ago, draftsmen began to draft provisions that were easier to read by dividing these long sentences into component passages and separating them by setting them out in 'paragraphs'. In statutes, as sections and subsections, and in documents, as clauses, subclauses, paragraphs and subparagraphs.

3.8.3   'Paragraphing'

Despite your best efforts, it will not always be possible to achieve the desired result in a legal document by use of short sentences. The interrelationship of sets of facts, conditions, qualifications and exceptions will need to be stated in such a way that the intended nexus between them is unambiguous. This cannot always be achieved with precision when expressed in a series of short sentences. Unfortunately this can result in very long and intricate sentences.

One remedy is to split a long sentence into short 'paragraphs' and 'subparagraphs'. When the complexity of the sentence is broken down in this way the eye helps the reader's mind to digest it.

Somewhat confusingly, the expression 'paragraph' is not being used here in its strict dictionary sense, but refers to a passage of text (which may or may not be a complete sentence) commencing on a new line and ending on a separate line to the text in the next passage. Each 'paragraph' is given a number or an initial letter and further subdivisions are usually marked by a distinguishing number or letter and successive indentation. Although it might have been desirable for this book to use an alternative expression for this technique, its use within the profession is so entrenched that you are bound to come across the word 'paragraph' being used in this way and it has therefore been adopted. When used in this sense, 'paragraph' appears in inverted commas.

Further confusion can be caused by the common use of the word to mean a particular level or subdivision of a clause (the status of which may differ from firm to firm). In this book, clauses are sub-divided according to the following hierarchy:

> clause;
> subclause;
> paragraph;
> subparagraph; and
> sub-subparagraph.

This is so whether or not a clause or subclause commences with introductory words and whether or not a 'paragraph' contains complete sentences.

Some firms arrange the subdivisions differently, making a distinction in nature between clauses, subclauses and sub-subclauses, on the one hand, and paragraphs, and subparagraphs on the other. Under this system, a *paragraph* is a sub-division of a *clause* where the clause begins with introductory words and the passage is not a complete sentence, i.e., where the clause is tabulated. Similarly, a subparagraph is a sub-division of a tabulated subclause. The hierarchy of subdivisions under this system is therefore:

clause;
paragraph (if tabulated);
subclause;
subparagraph (if tabulated);
sub-subclause.

Although this system helps to ensure that sentences are properly punctuated (clauses, subclauses etc. will always commence with a capital letter; paragraphs and subparagraphs with a lower-case letter), it can produce an unnecessarily complicated approach and an inelegant numbering system. For example, one firm which adopts this system uses decimal numbers for its clauses, subclauses and sub-subclauses, bracketed lower-case letters for its paragraphs and bracketed small roman numerals for its subparagraphs.

The system you adopt is largely a matter of personal taste. The overriding rule is: be clear on what the conventions are and use them consistently.

3.8.3.1 Advantages of subdivision by 'paragraphing'
Drafting in 'paragraphs' provides the draftsman with:

(a) the opportunity to divide and subdivide long sentences into short sentences, or parts of sentences, each part commencing a new line and standing out clearly;

(b) the ability to make cross-references with precision and economy of language; and

(c) the ability to isolate one or more particulars from a series and apply an exception or qualification.

3.8.3.2 Excessive subdivision
The technique of 'paragraphing' into successive subdivisions should not be taken too far. You will reach a stage where the structure of the clause becomes so complex that it detracts from the clarity and ease of communication which 'paragraphing' is intended to achieve. When this happens, you should rearrange your material. It is suggested that 'paragraphing' should go no further than the level of sub-subparagraphs.

3.8.4   Parts

If a document is particularly lengthy, it can be divided into parts
distinguished by capital letters or capital roman numerals. For example
'Part B' or 'Part II'. The use of capital letters is common in documents
numbered under the decimal system for example, 'B 3.5.7'. It is good
practice to assign a title to each part which should accurately and
logically group together the clauses within it. For example, loan
agreements are frequently divided into Part I – Introduction, Part II –
Interest, Part III – Payments, Part IV – Representations, Warranties and
Undertakings, Part V – Commissions, Fees and Charges, Part VI –
Default etc.

3.8.5   Numbering systems

3.8.5.1   Conventional system: 'alphanumeric'
Most draftsmen use a system involving a combination of arabic and
roman numbers and letters for clauses, subclauses, paragraphs and
subparagraphs. This system has the advantage that each level is
self-identifying. For example:

> Clauses (arabic numerals): 1, 2, 3 etc.
> Sub-clauses (bracketed capital letters): (A), (B), (C) etc.
> Paragraphs (bracketed roman numerals): (i), (ii), (iii) etc.
> Subparagraphs (bracketed lower-case letters): (a), (b), (c) etc.
> Subsubparagraphs (bracketed arabic numerals): (1), (2), (3) etc.

Subparagraph (f) of paragraph (iv) of subclause (C) of clause 17 is
represented:

> Subparagraph 17(C)(iv)(f).

3.8.5.2   Decimal system

An alternative method of distinguishing 'paragraphs' in a document is
the decimal system. Under this system a clause is given a number. The
subclauses within clause 1 are numbered 1.1, 1.2 etc. The subclauses
within clause 2 are numbered 2.1, 2.2 etc. The paragraphs in subclause
1.1 are numbered 1.1.1, 1.1.2 etc., and so on for subparagraphs and
sub-subparagraphs.

Subparagraph 6 of paragraph 4 of subclause 3 of clause 17 is represented:

Subparagraph 17.3.5.6.

This system has been adopted by many firms but it is still far from the prevailing system for documents. It is used more widely, however, in lengthy memoranda and in publications. It is the system adopted by Blackstone and is used throughout this book.

Of course, as a matter of principle, any system of numbering or lettering may be used, so long as it is used logically and consistently. It is essential that you apply the same pattern throughout the document.

3.8.6 Conventional arrangement

3.8.6.1 *Front sheet and contents page*
It is usual to attach a front sheet which sets out the date, the names of the parties, the title of the agreement and the name and address of the firm. In the case of draft documents it is good practice for the front sheet to include the word 'Draft', the number of that draft, the date the draft was prepared and the drafter's reference. In addition to marking the front sheet as a draft it is good practice to mark the first page of the document also.

Many documents benefit from the inclusion of a contents page which lists the clauses and operates as an index. There can be no rule of general application but a contents page will usually be appropriate for documents of five pages or more.

3.8.6.2 *Recitals*
Recitals are the introductory words or preamble in a deed or agreement and are traditionally introduced by the word 'WHEREAS' and each new recital begins 'AND WHEREAS'. The most radical modern practice is to use a heading such as 'Introduction' without a trace of 'recitals' or a 'whereas'. Others introduce the words with 'recitals' as a heading and dispense with the use of 'whereas'. Most firms compromise by using the title and a single introductory 'whereas' followed by numbered or lettered paragraphs.

Not all agreements need recitals. They are not intended to form an operative part of an agreement and should not contain operative provisions. They should be included only where background information is necessary to help the reader understand why the parties have decided to enter into the agreement. Commercial agreements usually recite earlier transactions and events leading to the agreement. Often even straightforward agreements contain an introductory recital about the transactions. For example, a share purchase agreement may have a single recital stating:

> WHEREAS the Vendors have agreed to sell to the Purchaser, and the Purchaser has agreed to purchase, the entire issued share capital of Intelligence Limited ('the Company') on the terms set out in this Agreement.

Sometimes, even though you might be happy to dispense with recitals altogether, others may insist upon them. One approach is to place the recitals in a schedule stating that the document is entered into having regard to the matters recited in the schedule. The material can then be drafted in a less formal style without the need for a single 'whereas'. On other occasions you may feel that some introductory statements are necessary for the document to be readily understood. In such a case it makes sense to place them at the beginning rather tuck them away in a schedule.

3.8.7 Expressions in block capitals

In addition to clause and schedule headings, which are usually typed in block capitals, there is a convention that certain expressions found in the formal parts of deeds, agreements and other documents also appear in this form. For example, the following words:

> 'THIS AGREEMENT' or 'THIS DEED';
> 'BETWEEN';
> 'WHEREAS';
> 'NOW THIS DEED WITNESSES';
> 'IT IS HEREBY AGREED'; and
> 'IN WITNESS WHEREOF'
> 'IT WAS RESOLVED THAT'.

Of itself, the practice is relatively harmless and, subject to any objection to archaic expression, if the forms or precedents you are using adopt this approach it is probably better to conform even if the appearance of these words in block capitals may seem somewhat eccentric to the lay client. In some documents it is also conventional to use block capitals for words signalling an exception or qualification in a 'proviso'. For example you will frequently find words such as:

'PROVIDED THAT';
'EXCEPT THAT'; and
'SUBJECT TO'

typed in block capitals.

3.8.8   Emboldening and underlining

Prudent and consistent use of emboldening or underlining to show the rank or importance of headings or text can have a considerable effect on a document's readability. It can also be used to highlight cross-references. However, its overuse can be self-defeating since its currency devalues the more you use it.

3.8.9   Headings and marginal notes

Headings are probably the most powerful layout device available to aid the readability of your document. Use headings liberally if they are accurate and helpful descriptions of sections of text.

Every clause should have a heading which describes succinctly what it is about so the reader may grasp the purpose of the clause and its subdivisions from the outset. It also enables a reader to locate quickly the clauses on a particular topic. If you divide your document into parts these too should have headings.

Many draftsmen add marginal notes indicating the function of the clause. Whilst they can be useful in a very long and detailed document or one with particularly lengthy clauses, they are generally unnecessary and merely clutter the page and add to the process of checking the draft. The need to give subclauses headings should generally also be avoided. It is usually better to create a new clause for each specific individual point being addressed. If you feel it is absolutely necessary to give subclauses headings in a document, make sure you do so consistently throughout the document.

Headings are usually underlined but not punctuated. Be careful not to overcrowd your writing with headings. Leaving ample space between headings and sections of text enables them to stand out as signposts for the reader's eye.

3.8.10   Cross-references

One of the advantages of drafting in 'paragraphs' is the opportunity to make cross-references with precision and economy of words. It enables you to refer to a paragraph as, say, 'paragraph (i) of subclause (A) of clause 3'. However, even this is an unnecessarily long-winded method. It is better to refer to 'clause 3(A)(i)' or, better still, to 'paragraph 3(A)(i)'. Either method is clear provided you are consistent but some regard the latter method, i.e. of referring in words to the lowest subdivision rather than to the clause, as better. This approach has the added advantage that it facilitates later reference to 'that paragraph'. If you use the expression 'clause 3(A)(i)' you cannot later say 'that clause' because you do not mean the whole clause nor can you say 'that paragraph' because it makes no sense in the context of the preceding words.

It is helpful to underline cross-references because they are then much easier to find if they need to be changed (as they often do). However, contrary to popular belief in some legal quarters, it is not a laudable achievement to maximise the number of cross-references in a document. Cross-references are a necessary evil. 'Evil' because, useful though they are, it is notoriously difficult to keep track of them by the time a document has gone through a number of drafts. Cross-references should therefore be kept to a minimum in order to maximise your chances of getting them right.

3.8.11   Page breaks

Pages should not end with a clause heading alone and, wherever possible, should end at a break between clauses or paragraphs. Schedules should commence on separate pages and should refer to the principal clause to which they relate.

3.9 THE CHOICE OF WORDS, PLAIN ENGLISH AND LEGAL MEANING

3.9.1 Principles of construction

Courts generally give words their dictionary meaning, usually referring to the *Oxford English Dictionary*. Where there is doubt, the primary rule of construction is that a document must be construed as a whole. Whilst they may be useful indicators, many earlier decisions as to the meaning of particular words are of limited value for this reason, since it is inescapable that the words will have been construed in a different context.

Although words repeated in a document will normally be given the same meaning throughout, there is no rule of construction of general application to this effect and the context may sometimes contribute significantly to the meaning given to an expression. For example, if in a partnership deed, the expression 'net profit' is used in one clause concerning salaries and the calculation of the sharing of profits and, in another, concerning payments to personal representatives in the event of a partner's death, it may be held to mean profits after the deduction of partners' salaries in the first provision but profits before deduction of salaries in the second provision (see *Watson* v *Haggitt* [1928] AC 127).

A detailed examination of the rules of interpretation is beyond the scope of this book but a basic appreciation is essential if you are to draft effectively. In particular, you should become familiar with the following established principles of construction:

(a) *Inclusio unius est exclusio alterius.* A provision expressed in specific or detailed terms will be taken to indicate an intention to exclude anything not falling within the specific words or detailed list.

(b) *Eiusdem generis.* Where general words follow specific words, the general words will be treated as restricted to the same class or category as the specific words. So a provision in a bill of lading referring to a port becoming 'unsafe in consequence of war, disturbance or any other cause' was held not to cover a port becoming unsafe by reason of ice conditions since it was not a cause *eiusdem generis* with war or disturbance (see *SS Knutsford Ltd* v *Tillmanns & Co.* [1908] AC 406).

(c)   *Noscitur a sociis*. Words associated with each other are construed on a common basis so that the scope of general words may be restricted to the context in which they are used.

(d)   *Contra proferentem*. Where a party relies upon an ambiguous provision, the ambiguity will be resolved by construing the provision against the interests of that party. At common law exclusion clauses are construed *contra proferentem*.

3.9.2   Intention of the parties

The court's approach to the intention of the parties is one of the most difficult aspects of law to explain to a client, whether at the time a document is prepared (in order to convince the client of the need to be complete and precise) or when advising on extant or potential litigation.

When a dispute arises over the meaning of the words used in a document, clients usually expect it to be resolved by reference to what they claim was the intention of the parties at the time of negotiations. Of course, there is no paramount rule of good faith in English law, allowing extrinsic evidence of contrary intention. Unless an exception to the parol evidence rule can be established, the courts will ascertain 'the expressed common intention' of the parties to a deed or agreement by looking only to the words actually used in the document. Similarly, although there are limited circumstances where extrinsic evidence may be admitted, the court will ascertain the meaning of a will by what the testator has actually written.

The House of Lords has, in recent years, established that 'the commercial, or business object of the transaction, objectively ascertained, may be a surrounding fact' to which the court should have regard, and rejected the idea that, as Lord Wilberforce put it, in *Prenn* v *Simmonds* [1971] 1 WLR 1381, 'English law is left behind in some island of literal interpretation'. Nevertheless, it remains clear that evidence of subjective intentions arising during pre-contractual negotiations is inadmissible.

This rule underlines the need for accuracy in drafting. You should always check that you understand the meaning which will be given by the courts to the words you intend to use and that your choice of words accurately reflects the intentions of your client. Never forget that the parties to a document will be presumed to have intended to say what in fact they said. The words you choose will be construed as they appear.

3.9.2.1 Non-literal interpretation

Sometimes parties, fearful that a court might defeat their intention by giving their document a strict literal interpretation, include a 'non-literal interpretation' clause. For example:

> This Agreement shall be interpreted, having regard to its underlying business purposes, in a reasonable and commercial manner rather than in strict accordance with the literal meaning of the language used.

Whilst similar clauses concerning interpretation by arbitrators have been upheld by the Court of Appeal, it is arguable that they provided the arbitrators in those cases no more liberty than provided by law.

If you feel such a clause may be appropriate in a particular case you should research the law thoroughly and select the words you use with great care.

3.9.2.2 Entire agreement clause

At the other end of the spectrum, a party may wish to ensure that no extrinsic evidence can be admitted under an exception to the parol evidence rule (e.g. where the written contract is claimed to be subject to an oral condition precedent), that the agreement represents the only agreement between the parties relating to the subject-matter, that it supersedes and extinguishes any other agreement between the same parties purporting to relate to the same subject-matter and that no claim can be brought on the grounds of misrepresentation or breach of collateral warranty. Despite considerable doubt concerning its general effectiveness (see the Law Commission Report No. 154 on the Parol Evidence Rule) and, in relation to misrepresentations, its chances of satisfying the requirements of reasonableness under the Unfair Contract Terms Act 1977, s. 11, it is increasingly common to see such clauses in contracts and other documents. A clause of this type might read:

> This Agreement constitutes the entire and only agreement between the parties relating to the [transactions provided for by this Agreement] and supersedes and extinguishes any prior drafts, agreements, undertakings, representations, warranties and arrangements of any nature, whether or not in writing, relating thereto.

Each party acknowledges that this Agreement has been entered into upon the terms set out in this Agreement and no reliance has been placed upon any representation, warranty, promise or assurance made or given by any person, whether or not in writing, other than those expressly contained in this Agreement.

3.9.3 Effect of recitals, headings, punctuation and layout

3.9.3.1   Recitals
Recitals may be taken into account in so far as they help to ascertain the meaning and effect of the document. A recital is often used to state that the agreement is 'supplemental to' an earlier agreement, for example:

WHEREAS this Agreement is supplemental to an agreement dated [   ] and made between the parties to this Agreement (the 'Principal Agreement') under which the Purchaser agreed to buy [   ] from the Vendor for [   ].

Since the Law of Property Act 1925, s. 58, provides that an instrument expressed to be supplemental to a previous instrument takes effect as if it contained 'a full recital of the previous instrument', statements about the effect of the previous instrument are usually unnecessary. However, it would seem that s. 58 is seldom relied on in practice and many recitals include references to the detailed provisions of another document.

Where recitals are included they should be drafted with great care as they may be used to indicate the intention of the parties if the operative provisions are found to be ambiguous, set up an estoppel or even create a distinct covenant.

3.9.3.2   Conflict between a recital and an operative clause
The well-established rules concerning how conflicts between recitals and operative clauses are to be resolved can be summarised as follows:

(a)   If the operative part of the deed is clear, and the recitals are not clear, the operative part prevails.

(b)   If the recitals are clear, but the operative part is ambiguous, the recitals control the operative part.

(c)   If the operative part and the recitals are both clear, but the one is inconsistent with the other, the operative part prevails.

See *Re Moon, ex parte Dawes* (1886) 17 QBD 275.

However, words in the operative part may be too general to be 'clear words' and be capable of being controlled by recitals. If, for example, the operative part of a power of attorney appoints solicitors as attorneys without limiting the duration of their powers but a recital states that the principal intends going abroad and desires the appointment of attorneys to act for him during his absence, the recital may be held to control the operative part and limit the powers to the duration of the principal's absence (see *Danby* v *Coutts & Co.* (1885) 29 ChD 500).

3.9.3.3   *A recital may set up an estoppel*

A recital is often justified on the basis that it might estop a party from denying something, for example, that a certain sum is due and owing from one party to another. For a recital to have this effect it must be clear and unambiguous and 'a distinct statement of a particular fact' (per Parke B in *Carpenter* v *Buller* (1841) 8 M & W 209 at p. 212). In many cases a more straightforward approach is to include in the operative clauses a representation or warranty as to that fact.

3.9.3.4   *Recital operating as a covenant or undertaking*

Where a deed contains an unqualified recital that one party is indebted to another for a specified amount, a covenant to pay will be implied if the sole object of the recital is to obtain an acknowledgement of the debt. This will not be so where the purpose of the recital was, for example, to state the debt on which the creation of a mortgage or a charge was to be based (*Jackson* v *North Eastern Railway Co.* (1877) 7 ChD 573 at pp. 582–7).

It has also been held possible for a recital to create a covenant where a deed recites that a particular party to it has agreed to do something but there is no covenant in the operative part. For example, in the absence of an express covenant in the operative part, a statement that the parties have agreed to live apart may be interpreted as mutual covenants that they will do so (see *Dawes* v *Tredwell* (1881) 18 ChD 354 at p. 358; and *Buckland* v *Buckland* [1900] 2 Ch 534).

3.9.3.5 Headings and marginal notes
The view expressed by Lord Reid in *Director of Public Prosecutions* v *Schildkamp* [1971] AC 1 that, in construing an Act, reference can be made to a cross-heading or to a marginal note probably applies equally to contracts and other private documents (possibly with more force since the objection that such headings are not debated by Parliament has no application). Lord Reid went on to say, however, that a heading or marginal note is a poor guide because it can do no more than indicate the main subject with which the section deals. It is thought, therefore, that whilst a heading in a contract or other private document may be referred to when construing a clause, it would not usually carry much weight and would rarely be decisive.

3.9.3.6 Excluding reference to headings
Nevertheless, it is normal for agreements to include a clause in the boilerplate which provides that headings are not to affect the interpretation of the document, such as:

No regard shall be had to the heading or title of any Part, clause or Schedule of this Agreement in construing any of its provisions;

or

The heading and marginal notes are for convenience only and do not affect the interpretation of this agreement.

3.9.3.7 Punctuation
The modern judicial attitude to the significance of punctuation in the interpretation of a document was discussed at 1.2.3. It seems likely that, where there is evidence that the parties used punctuation marks systematically throughout a private document, as an expression of their intention, a court will have regard to the punctuation where it makes clear which of two meanings is to be taken. However, if without the punctuation, the meaning is clear, the punctuation will be disregarded. For this reason you will often hear a lawyer say 'The words you use should carry the required meaning, even if they are unpunctuated.'

Many documents provide:

All marks of punctuation and brackets are to be deemed part of this document and are to be given full effect in interpreting it;

or, to the contrary,

> No regard shall be had to any marks of punctuation in this document in construing any of its provisions.

3.9.3.8 Layout

Similarly, it seems likely that a court, in interpreting a document which showed a systematic use of paragraphs and subparagraphs, numbering and indentation, would take layout devices into account.

3.10 EXPRESSIONS RELATING TO TIME

One of the most critical aspects of drafting is achieving precision with expressions relating to time. Frequently you will need to specify a time by which an act must be performed or an event must have happened; the exact date or time the relevant legal relationship is to commence or expire; the length of notice periods and so on. You should exercise great care with the phrases you use, taking time to check that their meaning exactly matches your intended result. The legal meaning of some expressions relating to time remains unclear. Wherever possible avoid them by using specific dates and times.

3.10.1 'From'

3.10.1.1 'From [a date]'

'From' a date probably means that the day of the specified date is *excluded* from the computation of time. However, this rule is not entirely clear from the authorities, being subject to dicta suggesting there is no absolute rule, and that it is a question of construction in each case (see per Warrington J in *English* v *Cliff* [1914] 2 Ch 376 at p. 382).

3.10.1.2 'From [an event / performance of an act]'

'From' the performance of an act or the happening of an event means that the day of performance, or the event happening, is prima facie *included* in computation of time.

It is probably better to use 'from and excluding' or 'from and including' or avoid 'from' altogether by referring to a period 'commencing on' or 'commencing with' a specified date (see below).

3.10.1.3   'From the date of this Agreement'

A distinct trap worth mentioning here (although it can arise whether 'from', 'on' or other such expression is used) arises where a clause specifies a period of time running from 'three months from the date hereof' or 'two years commencing on the date of this Agreement'. It has been held that the period is calculated by reference to the date inserted at the commencement of the Agreement even where that is not the date of true execution. It is better to avoid such expressions and refer instead to a period 'from and [including/excluding]' a specified date inserted in the document immediately before execution.

3.10.2   'On'

3.10.2.1   'On' a day

If a period of time is stated to begin on a named day, that day is included in the computation (*Sidebotham* v *Holland* [1895] 1 QB 378). Where performance is due on a particular day the party may perform up to midnight on that day (*Startup* v *Macdonald* (1843) 6 Man & G 593). If the day is a non-business day, then performance may be on the business day prior to the specified date. There are two exceptions to this rule. In the case of legal proceedings, when a party may take the required step on the next day that the courts are open for business. In the case of a bill of exchange, under the Bills of Exchange Act 1882, the payer is allowed to pay on the next business day (see also Banking and Financial Dealings Act 1971).

3.10.2.2   'On and from' or 'on and after' or 'on or before'

'On and from' or 'on and after' or 'on and before' a day *includes* that day (*Sidebotham* v *Holland* [1895] 1 QB 378 at p. 384). Where a person under an obligation to do a particular act has to do it 'on or before' a particular date he has the whole of that date to perform it. So where the obligation is to pay a sum into a bank account 'on or before' a particular date and payment is not received by the bank's close of business on that date, there is no default until midnight (*Afovos Shipping Co. SA* v *R. Pagnan and F. Lli* [1983] 1 WLR 195).

3.10.2.3   'Commencing on'

The specified day will be included in computing the period, so that a year 'commencing on' 1 May ends on the next 30 April (*Hare* v *Gocher* [1962] 2 QB 641).

3.10.3 'After', 'between' and the non-existent or non-distributed middle

3.10.3.1 'After'
Where a period (say three months) must expire *after* an event before something must be done, the date of that event is *not included* (*Browne v Black* [1912] 1 KB 316; *Williams v Burgess* (1840) 10 LJ QB 10). Adding 'from' to 'after' as in 'from and after' is redundant and does nothing to improve on the meaning of 'after'.

3.10.3.2 'Between [two dates]'
This expression will exclude both named dates from the computation.

3.10.3.3 The non-existent or non-distributed middle
This problem can arise in relation to expressions relating to time (as it can with money and measures of goods and the like).

The expression 'between [two dates]' is sometimes used where the intention is to isolate a particular day. Unfortunately an expression such as 'the period between 10 December and 11 December' is strictly meaningless because, both dates being excluded, there is no period. In many cases the context may enable a court to determine the parties' intentions but is unsafe to rely on this.

When 'after' and 'before' are used, both referring to the same date, an unintended hiatus may be caused. For example, 'whether before or after the date of this Agreement' will exclude the day of the agreement. A provision which applies one set of rules 'before 1 May' and another set 'after 1 May' will, on a strict interpretation, exclude 1 May from the application of either set of rules. If, for example, you wish the regulation of an existing legal relationship to change 'on' (or 'from and excluding' if that is the result you want) it is best to use that expression rather than a 'before/after' formulation. Otherwise make sure that either your 'before' or your 'after' is an 'on or [before / after]'.

3.10.4 'Within' and 'during'

3.10.4.1 'Within'
'Within [so many] days after [an event]' will not usually include the day of the happening of the event (*Williams v Burgess* (1840) 10 LJ QB 10). For example, if the document says: 'Within seven days after [an event]',

and the event happens on 1 June, the period ends at midnight of 8/9 June. It is best to avoid doubt by using an expression which states precisely when the period begins. For example: 'within a period of three months commencing on [...] '.

3.10.4.2 *'During'*
The expression 'during' a stated time should not be used to mean 'in the course of that time' but in its strict legal sense, to mean 'throughout the whole time'; not for 'from time to time' in a period but 'persisting for the whole period' (see *R* v *Inhabitants of Anderson* (1846) 9 QB 663 at p. 668).

3.10.5 'Till', 'until', 'to' and 'by [a day]'

3.10.5.1 *'Till', 'until'*
'Till' and 'until' a day, are both ambiguous as to whether the day is included. It is better to say 'until and including 1 April 1993' or 'until but not including . . .'.

3.10.5.2 *'To'*
Similarly, it is ambiguous to say, 'from 1 April to 5 May'. It is better to say 'from 1 April to 5 May, both days [included/excluded]'.

3.10.5.3 *'By [a day]'*
An act to be done 'by' a specified date may be performed on or at any time before that date. 'On or before' is preferable.

3.10.6 'Day', 'Days'

3.10.6.1 *'Day'*
A day is 24 consecutive hours, usually from midnight to the following midnight but *may* mean 24 hours commencing at a particular hour or time if the intention is expressed clearly. For example, a motor insurance policy commonly begins at noon on one day and ends at noon on another. If there is any possibility of doubt make it clear by being specific.

If you want a period to be measured in whole days, the period should be stated to 'commence on' or 'commence with' a specified or ascertainable day, not a specified or ascertainable time. Some take the view that the use of the word 'time' or equivalent expression suggests that the period is to be measured from a precise time of the day. Similarly, if an *event* is specified, without mention of the 'day', time may begin to run from the exact time of the happening of the event.

3.10.6.2 *'Quarter days'*
The four 'quarter days' are the four 'feast days': Lady Day (25 March), Midsummer Day (24 June), Michaelmas Day (29 September) and Christmas Day (25 December). 'Half quarter days' fall on 2 February, 9 May, 11 August and 11 November.

3.10.6.3 *'Working days' or 'business days'*
Days are generally consecutive days. In view of this banking and other commercial documents normally contain special provisions designed to ensure that parties can perform, and periods can end, only on days on which banks and financial markets are open in the relevant financial centres. Whilst you or your firm may not have an international finance practice, the same considerations can apply to more domestic matters. You should always consider whether an expression such as 'working days' or 'business days' would be more appropriate.

3.10.6.4 *'Clear days'*
A 'clear day' is a period of 24 hours commencing at midnight. So 'within 14 clear days after 1 May' means the period commencing at midnight of 1/2 May and ending at midnight on 15/16 May.

3.10.6.5 *'At least', 'not less than' [a specified number of days]*
'Not less than 14 days' has been held to mean an interval of at least 14 *clear* days, i.e. 14 complete days must intervene or elapse. If you provide, for example, that 'not less than 21 days' notice' is required for a meeting, you will exclude the day of service of notice and the day of the meeting itself (*Re Hector Whaling Ltd* [1936] Ch 208; *Thompson* v *Stimpson* [1961] 1 QB 195). Similarly, 'at least seven days' will be taken as seven clear days.

If you intend to compute in complete days it is always best to *state* whether or not you intend them to be 'clear' days.

3.10.7 'Weeks', 'months' and 'years'

3.10.7.1 *'Week'*
A week will normally be calculated from midnight Saturday to midnight on the following Saturday. However, if you choose to define the

expression yourself it may be defined as running from midnight of any specified day of the week, or date, to midnight seven days later.

3.10.7.2 'Month'

At common law 'month' normally meant lunar month except in the case of bills of exchange and certain other commercial documents where it meant a calendar month. Although the Law of Property Act 1925, s. 61, provides that month means 'calendar month', it is best to include it specifically in the definitions clause. If you intend a month to be a lunar month or some other variation, it is essential to include a definition, for example, 'a month means a period of 28 days'.

Where the calendar month definition applies and where the period of a month, or a specified number of months, is to be calculated from a specified date in a month, the period expires on the corresponding date of the succeeding or last month in the period, so that performance will be due or the notice will expire on that same day each succeeding month. However, because the number of days in five of the months of the year is less than in the seven others the corresponding-date rule is that one month's notice given in a 30-day month is one day shorter than one month's notice given in a 31-day month and is three days shorter if it is given in February. When the day is the 29th, 30th or 31st and the 'end' month has only 28 days, or, where the day is the 31st, and the 'end' month has only 30 days the date of performance or expiry will be the last day of the month (see *Dodds* v *Walker* [1981] 1 WLR 1027).

3.10.7.3 'Year'

The judicially accepted meaning of 'year' is altogether unsurprising. It means a period of 12 calendar months calculated either from 1 January or from some other named day and consists of 365 days in an ordinary year and 366 days if the period includes 29 February in a leap year. In the absence of provision to the contrary a 'year' will be taken to mean a calendar year of 1 January to 31 December. If you wish your year to be a 12-month period running from a chosen date you must say so expressly.

3.10.8 'Forthwith', 'immediately', 'reasonable time', 'as soon as possible'

3.10.8.1 'Forthwith', 'immediately'

Both words mean that an act must be done without delay and as soon as possible in the circumstances, having regard to the nature of the act to be done. Wherever possible, it is preferable to be specific by stating the required period expressly. Sometimes it is not possible or desirable to be specific and such an expression is appropriate. In such cases, since there appears to be no material difference in meaning between 'forthwith' and 'immediately', it is suggested that you pass over the archaic 'forthwith' in favour of the more modern 'immediately'.

3.10.8.2   '[Within] a reasonable time'
This means a reasonable time under ordinary circumstances interpreted as a question of fact. There is no automatic relief from delays caused by unforeseen problems. Again, it is preferable to be specific unless this is impossible or the client's interests are better served by a more vague formulation. It can be a very costly business to have the House of Lords determine what a reasonable period was in a particular case (see *Stickney* v *Keeble* [1915] AC 386).

3.10.8.3   'As soon as possible'
'As soon as possible' means within a reasonable and the shortest practicable time. Although surrounding circumstances may be relevant, the limited resources of the party giving the undertaking will not be taken into account. You should therefore resist any suggestion that your client undertake to perform an act 'as soon as possible'.

3.11   DEFINITIONS

Definitions are among the most difficult provisions to draft and great care is needed. The consequences of a flawed definition can be far-reaching. Each time the defined term is used your client may be exposed to potential unintended results.

The correct approach to the use of definitions is to use them only where there would be doubt without them. Do not overuse definitions. In particular do not attempt to define words where their everyday or obvious sense is clear or where words already carry the desired meaning by virtue of an Act of Parliament or judicial interpretation. The only exception to this is where you wish to inform readers of the meaning the law will give to an expression.

3.11.1   General matters

3.11.1.1   Location and isolation of definitions
Generally, definitions are best included in an interpretation or 'dictionary' clause as clause 1 in an agreement and should be listed in alphabetical order. Occasionally it may be preferable to include a particular definition in a schedule if it is particularly lengthy or complex or even all definitions if there are a great number of them. In the former case, the defined word or expression should nonetheless be referred to in the interpretation clause. For example:

'Notice of Drawing' means a notice in the form set out in Schedule 2.

'Running' definitions, i.e. definitions appearing in the particular operative clauses to which they relate (or the first of such operative clauses), should be used only in short, simple documents where an entire clause devoted to interpretation would be excessive and cumbersome or where the definition can be relevant only to the clause or group of clauses in which it appears. In the latter case, the defined word should nonetheless be referred to in the interpretation clause or definitions schedule. For example:

'*Force Majeure*' has the meaning given in clause 14(A) (*force majeure*).

Most lawyers underline defined terms where they first occur in a document and to give them initial capital letters wherever they occur. This is for ease of reference and to remind the reader that the word is a defined term. However, this convention is often criticised by the advocates of plain English. It can certainly give a document an odd appearance and, on close examination, it is perhaps questionable whether it really does serve a useful purpose. A competent lawyer reading a document will always examine the definitions clause carefully. It is at least arguable that, providing you use sufficiently distinctive definitions, the device of using initial capital letters should be unnecessary.

Nevertheless, the convention is deeply entrenched in the profession and it is thought that the practice can be helpful when used sensibly, but in documents commonly read by non-lawyers, such as articles of association or consumer credit agreements, the use of capital letters should be confined to a minimum.

Do not use definitions as operative clauses of a document with exceptions and undertakings built in. This can often happen as a result of negotiated revisions to a draft. Where this happens it is better to take the negotiated draft and redraft it with a separate undertaking and place the definition in the interpretation clause. Similarly, do not hide substantive provisions within an interpretation clause. For example:

> 'Completion Date' means 1 May 1993, on which date the Purchaser shall pay the Purchase Price.

3.11.1.2   Inclusion of the definite or indefinite article in a definition

The decision whether to include the definite or indefinite article in a defined term can have important consequences. Make sure that it is a conscious decision. It is generally better to exclude the definite or indefinite article. Where it is included the use of the defined term can become awkward grammatically and can cause dangerous confusion if there is any possibility of your using the same expression in a non-specific way. For example, if a company is defined as 'the Company' and there is later reference to another company referred to as 'the company' the parties' intention may be unclear.

3.11.1.3   Flawed definitions

One of the most common problems arises where the draftsman, having defined the term with certain provisions in mind, fails to contemplate the impact of the definition on other provisions. The definition may produce the desired result in most clauses but be too general or too restricted when applied to others. Where the defined term does not fit a particular context you should redefine the term to accommodate it, select another expression for use in the particular context or restrict the application of your definition to particular contexts.

Although generally frowned upon as an undesirable expression, particularly with letters, the phrase 'in relation to' is commonly used in statutes and in private documents to make it clear that a definition applies to the defined term only in a particular context. For example:

> In this part 'author', in relation to a work, means the person who creates it (Copyright, Designs and Patents Act 1988, s. 9(1)).

It is a laborious but essential task to check your document to ensure that each definition produces no anomalous results in any of the clauses in which it appears. If you follow the suggestion above on planning definitions and check your document for each use of the defined expression, deciding in each case whether the expression as defined fits the context, you will eliminate many potential problems of this kind.

3.11.1.4 'Except where the context otherwise requires'
An interpretation clause is commonly introduced by this or one of a number of such expressions, as illustrated below:

> In this Agreement, [unless a contrary intention appears]; [except where the context otherwise requires]; [unless inconsistent with the context or subject matter]; or [where the context so admits]:

Such phrases are intended to guard against errors resulting from a word being used in a sense other than the one defined. This may easily occur where the word you have chosen as your defined term has more than one common meaning or a single common usage other than the sense defined. The purpose of the provision to allow an ordinary meaning to be given to a word where the context clearly shows this was intended by disapplying an otherwise automatic and overriding definition. An expression of this kind is not intended, and is unlikely, to afford complete protection against the consequences of the more serious error described above.

Even so some argue that there should be no need for these expressions, asserting that they are 'lazy devices for lazy draftsmen' who fail to consider their drafts with sufficient care. Of course, great care should be taken over each definition you choose. However, with long documents where negotiations have resulted in a number of revisions (and where others may have had an imput into the draft) it is not easy to be so sure that errors of this kind have not slipped in. Provided you have checked the document thoroughly and you have not used such an expression through laziness, phrases such as 'where the context so admits' do no harm and act as a final fail-safe.

3.11.1.5 Mathematical expressions
Where mathematical calculations are involved it is permissible and often desirable to use algebraic formulae. Lawyers are rarely as confident with

figures as they are with words and since words will generally prevail over figures it is best to 'spell it out in words' in addition to the mathematical version of the equation or formula.

Many financial and commercial agreements contain provisions describing arithmetical concepts. For example, loan agreements permitting prepayment commonly have provisions incorporating complex arithmetical formulae for computing the sum to be paid by the borrower in such an event.

A good example of the use of such arithmetical expression can be found in the Taxation of Chargeable Gains Act 1992, s. 42(2), describing the method for computing a gain or a loss on the occasion of a part disposal of an asset.

As with expressions relating to time, beware the 'non-distributed middle' in relation to weights, measures, payments or charges. When using 'less than/more than' type formulations it is possible to leave a hiatus. For example:

> Where the profits are less than £8 million the consideration shall be equal to [. . .].

> Where the profits are more than £8 million the consideration shall be equal to [. . .].

It is best to use formulations such as 'up to and including', 'exceeding [Y]' or 'exceeding [Y] but not exceeding [X]'.

3.11.2 Abbreviation using 'nicknames'

Abbreviation or giving a 'nickname' helps to ensure consistency and relieve the repetition of a lengthy phrase. By giving a short name to a long phrase you can avoid wholesale repetition. The traditional method is to state the expression to be abbreviated, e.g. 'John Norman Edwards and Peter James Harding', followed by the words 'hereinafter referred to as' (or 'in this Agreement called' or simply 'called'), e.g., 'the Vendors'.

The modern approach is preferable because it is shorter and dispenses with the verbose and archaic 'hereinafter'. The first time you use the expression to be abbreviated follow it with the abbreviation in quotation marks and contain it within brackets. For example:

> Amalgamated Cake and Biscuit Manufacturers (Holdings) plc (the 'Company').

As illustrated above, rather than repeat the names of the parties to a transaction, it is usual practice to give them 'nicknames' which describe them in terms appropriate to their connection with the transaction, for example:

> 'The trustees' means the trustees for the time being of the settlement.

It is almost always possible to contrive a 'nickname' but where no apt word can be found to describe a person mentioned repeatedly in the document, it may be appropriate to abbreviate the name when it first occurs. For example, '(called "Mr Ralphs")'. This avoids the necessity to repeat the Christian names and reduces the temptation to use 'the said'.

Another common use of nicknames is in relation to real property, once again, principally to avoid needless repetition:

> The 'Demised Premises' means the ground floor and garden at the Garden Flat, 34a Park Gate Drive, Hampton-on-Tweed, Oxbridgeshire, shown as red on the plan.

But since the principal purpose of a nickname is to abbreviate, the name ought to be the shortest available, providing it is sufficiently descriptive. Instead of the expression 'Demised Premises', you could drop the archaic 'demised' to leave the 'Premises' or use the simple and unstuffy, 'Garden Flat'. Providing your definition is comprehensive and accurate you can use any appropriate nickname.

Do not use nicknames for the sake of it. Sadly, the following example is found too often:

> The lease, hereinafter called 'the Lease'.

3.11.3 Stipulative definitions

Whilst nicknames are simply convenient abbreviations, used principally for their brevity and rarely to achieve a specific legal result, other types of definition can give a particular meaning to a word, or clarify, extend or restrict the word's dictionary meaning. A definition which extends or restricts that meaning is sometimes called a 'stipulative' definition.

Stipulative definitions can either be 'closed-ended' or 'open-ended'.

3.11.3.1 'Closed-ended' or 'means'-type definitions
The 'closed-ended' definition will usually (but not necessarily) use the word 'means' (or 'is/are') followed by a single definition or a list. Where you use a definition of this type you are saying that the definition given is complete and comprehensive and the defined term is not open to any other meaning or shade of meaning. It restricts the scope of the term by specifying *all* the items, circumstances etc. covered by it. As a by-product it often acts as an abbreviation or nickname where a multiple-word phrase would otherwise be repeated throughout the document.

'Business day' means a day on which banks and foreign exchange markets are in for business in London and New York.

'Proceedings' means any proceedings before a court or tribunal (including an arbitration) whether in England or elsewhere.

'Security interest' means any mortgage, charge, pledge or lien.

'Directors' means the directors of the Company for the time being.

A time of day is, unless otherwise stated, a reference to London time.

The main advantage of using a closed-ended definition is that it promotes certainty. Its principal disadvantage is that the rule of construction, *inclusio unius est exclusio alterius*, will apply so that the defined term will not cover items, circumstances etc. not mentioned in the definition.

3.11.3.2 'Open-ended' or 'includes'-type definitions
An open-ended definition is usually (but not necessarily) introduced by the word 'includes' followed by a list. This formulation is used to clarify the meaning of a defined term by giving examples but attempting to leave open the possibility of other items or circumstances falling within it. For example:

'Expenses' includes costs, charges and expenses of every description.

'Notice' includes a demand, consent or waiver.

An open-ended definition is also commonly used to widen an expression's ordinary or technical meaning to include an item which it would not normally cover. When you use a definition of this type in this way, you are saying that the defined term has its ordinary meaning *plus* something it would not ordinarily mean. For example:

'Hire-purchase agreement' includes conditional sale, chattel leasing and retention of title agreements.

'Literary work' includes a written table or compilation.

'Noise' includes vibration.

A variant of this type of definition is to invert it so that it restricts the meaning of a term. For example:

'Dwellinghouse' does not include a caravan or other mobile home.

A combination definition includes some items and excludes others:

'Goods' include all personal chattels other than things in action and money.

'Company' includes any body corporate or unincorporated association but does not include a partnership.

3.11.3.3 'Means and includes'?
The expression 'means' and 'includes' should never be combined. You will sometimes see this expression used by draftsmen who have failed to consider the mutually exclusive nature of the two types of definition. The combined expression does not remove the disadvantages of either expression when used alone and probably has the same effect as 'means' but it will be a (difficult) question of construction in every case.

The main disadvantage of open-ended definitions is that they expose the definition to a degree of uncertainty. Their principal advantage is that by doing so they stand a chance of covering something which though not included in the list is within the spirit, if not the letter, of the definition.

Open-ended definitions often end with expressions such as 'or any other
...'. If you wish to avoid the *eiusdem generis* rule you should consider
adding an expression such as 'whether or not similar to any of the
foregoing'.

Sometimes it may be appropriate in an open-ended definition to provide
a particular example following more general examples. For example:

> 'Goods' include all personal chattels other than things in action and
> money ...; and in particular 'goods' includes emblements, industrial
> growing crops, and things attached to or forming part of the land which
> are agreed to be severed before sale or under the contract of sale.

However, where general words are followed by a particular example, the
courts may apply the *inclusio unius est exclusio alterius* rule to limit the
generality of the words preceding the particular example. Where an
'includes ... and in particular includes ...' formulation is used it is often
accompanied by the words 'without prejudice to the generality of the
foregoing'. Even where there is no 'particular' example but where the items
included in the definition cover only the main examples of the defined term,
it is common to see the expression 'but is not limited' used. For example:

> 'Mortgage' includes, but is not limited to, a charge or lien on real or
> personal properties to secure money.

3.11.4 Statutory definitions

Make maximum use of definitions contained in Acts of Parliament.
Statutory definitions fall into one of two categories: definitions which
apply automatically unless excluded and definitions which can be
expressly adopted.

3.11.4.1 Automatically applied definitions
For example, under the Law of Property Act 1925, s. 61, in any deed,
contract or other instrument governed by English law:

  (a)   'month' means calendar month;
  (b)   'person' includes a corporation;
  (c)   the singular includes the plural and vice versa; and
  (d)   the masculine includes the feminine and vice versa.

You may sometimes see the expression: 'Person or persons corporation or corporations'. The use of both singular and plural for corporations and persons is quite unnecessary, as is the use of corporation. It is sufficient to use either 'person' or 'persons' (which sometimes suits the context more appropriately than 'person').

Where you intend to make a provision apply only to natural persons, the term 'individual' should be used instead of 'person'. The definition of 'person' in s. 61 is narrower than the definition in the Interpretation Act 1978 which includes a body of persons unincorporate. Where you wish to include unincorporated associations, it is best to provide a definition of 'person' which expressly incorporates the definition in the Interpretation Act 1978. Sometimes it is necessary to define 'person' more fully, usually to ensure that bodies such as the Panel on Takeovers and Mergers, certain types of joint venture vehicle and the like which might otherwise be classified as not having legal personality, are included. In such cases a detailed definition should be drafted, tailored to the particular circumstances.

3.11.4.2   Adoption of a statutory definition

You may wish to adopt a convenient definition contained in a statute. Remember that, even though a statute contains an appropriate and widely adopted definition for an expression it is relatively rare for it to apply that definition to private documents. It is a common error to assume that a definition contained in, for example, the Interpretation Act 1978 will apply to the document. You will usually find that it is necessary to incorporate such a definition expressly. In practice, you will find that words and expressions that feature recurrently in documents are, by tradition, given definitions based on a particular statutory provision. Here are some examples:

> 'Control', in relation to a company or partnership, has the meaning given in section 840 of the Income and Corporation Taxes Act 1988.

> 'Holding company' has the meaning given in section 736 of the Companies Act 1985.

> 'Land' has the meaning given in schedule 1 to the Interpretation Act 1978.

> 'Personal representative' has the meaning given in section 272 of the Inheritance Tax Act 1984.

'Securities' has the meaning given in section 228(6) of the Companies Act 1985.

'Subsidiary' has the meaning given in section 736 of the Companies Act 1985.

'Undertaking' has the meaning given in section 259 of the Companies Act 1985.

Whilst statutory definitions provide a catalogue of useful defined terms, never incorporate one without first checking carefully that it provides the right definition for your document. For example, in geographical definitions, if you intend to include the Isle of Man and the Channel Islands you may, of course, give 'United Kingdom' a wider definition but it is better to use the expression 'British Islands' and expressly adopt the definition in the Interpretation Act 1978. Do not restrict your document to 'England' when you mean 'England and Wales'. Use that expression and expressly incorporate the statutory definition. Since neither the Laws in Wales Act 1535 nor the Union with Scotland Act 1706 restrict their definitions to Acts of Parliament, it would seem that the expression 'Great Britain' may not need an express definition. If you are left in any doubt it is best to provide one.

Geographical statutory definitions

'British Islands'	United Kingdom, the Channel Islands and the Isle of Man	Interpretation Act 1978, s. 5 and sch. 1.
'United Kingdom'	Great Britain and Northern Ireland	Interpretation Act 1978, sch. 1.
'Great Britain'	England, Wales and Scotland	Laws in Wales Act 1535; Union with Scotland Act 1706; Wales and Berwick Act 1746.
'England'	Counties of England, Greater London and the Isles of Scilly	Local Government Act 1972; Interpretation Act 1978, sch. 1.
'Wales'	Counties of Wales	Local Government Act 1972, s. 20; Interpretation Act 1978, sch. 1.

3.11.4.3   'As amended'

Where a document refers to a statute the courts have refused to recognise a presumption that the parties intended it to refer to the statute in its amended form. Further, although the Interpretation Act 1978, s. 17(2)(a) (the only provision of the Act which automatically applies to deeds and agreements), provides that a reference in any deed or agreement to an original Act includes a reference to a subsequent Act, it only applies if that subsequent Act repeals, as well as re-enacts the original Act. It is therefore usual to see an agreement, containing references to statutory provisions, also contain an 'as amended' provision within the interpretation clause. For example:

> In this Agreement any reference to an enactment or statutory instrument includes a reference to it as amended (whether before or after the date of this Agreement) and to any other enactment which may, after the date of this Agreement, directly or indirectly replace it, with or without amendment.

The effect of the provision is to alter the contract's terms automatically if any of the statutory provisions referred to are subsequently amended. For example, in a document containing a definition of 'subsidiary' which adopts by reference the definition in the Companies Act 1985, s. 736, the definition would have been amended automatically when the Companies Act 1989, s. 144, came into force. If, on the other hand, the document defined 'subsidiary' by using the same definition as the one contained in the original s. 736 but made no reference to the section or the Act, an 'as amended' clause would have no effect and the original definition would remain.

3.12   DELIBERATE USE OF UNDEFINED OR IMPRECISE WORDS AND THE BURDEN OF PROOF

In most cases it is best to be specific wherever possible. However, it is sometimes either impossible or inappropriate to be specific where there is some uncertainty surrounding the subject-matter. For example, the subject-matter may have 'dynamic' characteristics which make it difficult to set a definition capable of surviving new developments. In such cases the problem may be solved by a statement that the parties intend an expression to be interpreted in accordance with the accepted practice of leading practitioners engaged in the relevant business or activity.

Alternatively, it may be desirable not to attempt precision preferring a use of words which indicates the parties' intention but leaves the precise meaning to be determined by the court. The classic example of such a word is 'reasonable'. The courts are generally happy to determine whether or not actions, omissions, time periods and the like are, or were. 'reasonable'.

If you decide that it is appropriate to leave a term undefined or to use an imprecise expression be careful not to be so vague as to render your clause or document void for uncertainty.

3.12.1 'Sufficient', 'material' and 'knowingly'

Expressions such as these are common and, at first sight, seem unobjectionable. Whilst the use of such words may serve the purpose of conveniently, and sometimes tactfully, watering down a provision which might otherwise seem Draconian, they raise questions that can be difficult to answer. Is 'knowledge' to be restricted to actual knowledge or does it include constructive knowledge? 'Sufficient' for whose purposes? 'Material' to whom and in what circumstances?

Where these and other similar expressions have been used by experienced lawyers you will often see apparent 'softeners' such as 'material' qualified by words such as 'in the opinion of the bank'.

3.12.2 'Substantial'

There have been many landlord and tenant cases concerning expressions such as 'substantial part of the rent' where the courts have been prepared to determine, as a matter of fact in each case, whether or not performance was substantial or not (*Palser v Grinling* [1948] 1 All ER 1; *Artillery Mansions Ltd v Macartney* [1949] 1 KB 164).

The expression 'substantial' is found in many agreements. For example. there is commonly a clause in a loan agreement which prohibits the borrower from selling or disposing of the 'whole or a substantial part of its assets'. The courts have refused to accept the argument that such clauses are void for uncertainty (*Commercial Union Assurance Co. Ltd v Tickler Ltd* (4 March 1959) unreported).

3.12.3 Burden of proof

Certain facts can be very difficult to prove. The practical difficulties of proving a breach governed by words such as 'sufficient', 'material' or 'knowingly' reduces significantly the value of the undertaking to the party receiving it. It is therefore common to see provisions which attempt to assist a party to discharge the burden of proof. You may see a provision that deems a determination or certificate issued by an identified person or expert to be 'prima facie', or even 'conclusive', evidence of the facts to be proved. Alternatively, you may find yourself arguing for or against (depending on your client's position) a provision which shifts the burden of proof by providing that the facts in question will be 'presumed unless the contrary is proved'.

3.13 STANDARDS OF OBLIGATION: 'BEST' AND 'REASONABLE' ENDEAVOURS

Your client will not wish to undertake all the obligations in a document in absolute or unqualified terms, especially if performing an obligation depends upon factors outside the client's control, for example, authorisation or consent must be obtained from a third party.

A strict undertaking expressed as 'shall . . .' may be diluted in degrees from 'shall do his utmost to . . .' through 'shall use his best endeavours to . . .' to 'shall use reasonable endeavours'.

The principal distinction between 'best' and 'reasonable endeavours' appears to be that 'reasonable endeavours' permits a party to consider commercial implications before complying with an obligation (*UBH (Mechanical Services) Ltd v Standard Life Assurance Co.* (1986) *The Times*, 13 November 1986), whereas an undertaking to use best endeavours might require a party to ignore some commercial considerations (*IBM United Kingdom Ltd v Rockware Glass Ltd* [1980] FSR 335). For example, whereas 'best endeavours' will usually (but see, for example, *Rackham v Peak Foods Ltd* [1990] BCLC 895; *John Crowther Group plc v Carpets International plc* [1990] BCLC 460) require a party to commence legal proceedings if litigation has a reasonable chance of success, undertaking to use 'reasonable endeavours' may permit a party to decide not to resort to litigation having considered the uncertainties of litigation or the effects of litigation on commercial relationships.

Your client incurs a heavy obligation by agreeing to use 'best endeavours'. Even the preferred expression 'reasonable endeavours' is not free from risk. It is usually best to try to specify the precise nature of the obligation which your client is prepared to undertake.

3.14   SENTENCES AND PARAGRAPHS

As with all good writing, a provision in a legal document should not deal with more than one idea. Two or more disconnected ideas require separate sentences or paragraphs.

At the planning stage you will have arranged your material under main and subheadings. These may themselves conveniently equate with clause headings. If they contain several themes, separate each theme into a clause heading of its own.

Where you have a choice, it is always better to use short, simple sentences. It follows from the points made in the paragraph above that, wherever possible, you should split a long sentence into two or more short sentences.

Some provisions can be expressed simply and in short sentences. Sometimes an entire clause may be dispensed with in one sentence of 15 to 30 words. For example:

Time of Essence
Save as otherwise expressly provided, time is of the essence of this Agreement.

Costs and Expenses
Save as otherwise stated in this Agreement, each party shall pay its own costs and expenses in relation to the negotiation, preparation, execution and carrying into effect of this Agreement.

Choice of Governing Law
This Agreement is governed by and shall be construed in accordance
with English law.

However, it is not always possible to achieve the desired result in a legal
document by use of short sentences. The interrelationship of sets of facts,
conditions, qualifications and exceptions will need to be stated in such a
way that the intended nexus between them is unambiguous. Precision
cannot always be achieved in a series of short simple sentences.

The solution to this problem is to adopt a strictly logical approach to
sentence structure and to break a complicated clause into simple
component parts set out using the 'paragraphing' technique.

3.14.1   Paragraphing

One way to relieve a long sentence is to split it into short 'paragraphs' and
'subparagraphs'. The complexity of the sentence is then broken down in
a way that makes it more easy to digest.

The arrangement of a clause into 'paragraphs' usually takes one of three
forms:

(a)   The sentences that make up the clause may be arranged in-
numbered or lettered subclauses. For example:

FORCE MAJEURE

(1)   '*Force Majeure*' means, in relation to either party, a circum-
      stance beyond the reasonable control of that party.

(2)   Neither party to this agreement shall be deemed to be in breach
      of this agreement or otherwise liable to the other for any delay in
      performance or for any non-performance of any obligations
      under this agreement to the extent that the delay or non-
      performance is due to *Force Majeure* and the time for perform-
      ance of that obligation shall be extended accordingly.

(3)   If a party's performance of its obligations under this agreement is
      affected by *Force Majeure*, it shall promptly notify the other

party of the nature and extent of the circumstances giving rise to *Force Majeure*.

(b) The clause may begin with an introductory sentence upon which the remainder depends, the remaining material being set out in numbered or lettered 'paragraphs' each consisting of separate complete sentences. For example:

TERMINATION

The following provisions apply to the termination of this Lease.

(1) The Lessee may by giving not less than one month's notice in writing. . . .

(2) If at any time during the term of this Lease the goods or any part thereof ceases to have any further useful life. . . .

(c) The continuity of a single sentence may be kept by using introductory words followed by numbered or lettered 'paragraphs' each ending in a comma or semicolon except the last which should end with a full stop unless your wish to use concluding words which continue from the introductory words. When isolated from other intermediate 'paragraphs', each 'paragraph' should be capable of forming a grammatical sentence with the introductory and any concluding material. For example:

NOTICES

Any notice or other communication given or made under or in connection with this agreement shall be in writing and shall be addressed [ ] and, if so addressed, shall be deemed to have been duly given or made as follows:

(1) if sent by personal delivery, upon delivery to [address];

(2) if sent by first-class post, two Business Days after the date of posting; and

(3) if sent by facsimile, when dispatched

PROVIDED THAT if, in accordance with the above provisions, any such notice or other communication would otherwise be deemed to be given or made outside Working Hours, such notice or other communication shall be deemed to be given or made at the start of Working Hours on the next Business Day.

3.14.2   The logic of the legal sentence

How should the parts of a legal sentence be arranged? Some guidance can be obtained from a treatise 'On legislative expression; or the language of the written law'. It was written by George Coode, a barrister of the Inner Temple, in an introduction to the appendix to the *Report of the Poor Law Commissioners on Local Taxation*, which was presented to Parliament in 1843. The Appendix, compiled according to the principles explained in the introduction, consisted of a digest of the entire statute law relating to the subject.

3.14.2.1   Coode's rule
Coode's rule says that every law has up to four elements. A legislative sentence essentially consists of the description of the *legal subject* (the person permitted or commanded to act) and the enunciation of the *legal action* (that which the subject is permitted or commanded to do).

Where the law in question is not of universal application, two further ingredients are added, the description of the *case* to which the legal action is confined (i.e. the circumstances in which the rule is to operate) and the *condition* on performance of which the legal action operates.

Although this rule was enunciated in relation to legislative drafting it is equally applicable to the drafting of any legal document. In the context of private documents, substitute 'legal sentence' for 'law' and 'legislative sentence'.

3.14.2.2   Sentence order
In most instances a legal sentence should be arranged in the following order:

(a)   the case,

(b)   the condition,

(c)   the legal subject, and

(d)   the legal action.

Coode gives an example:

> Where there is any question between any parishes touching the boundaries of such parishes (the case), if a majority of not less than two-thirds in number and value of the landowners of such parishes make application in writing (the condition), the Tithe Commissioners for England and Wales (the legal subject), may deal with any dispute or question concerning such boundaries (the legal action).

If you follow this rule of systematic presentation it will assist you to order your ideas and assist your readers to understand the meaning of your draft.

Suppose you were instructed to draft an agency agreement under which one party (the 'Hirer') is to act as agent for your client (the 'Lessor') for the purpose of purchasing plant, machinery and equipment which your client is then to supply under a lease to the hirer. Your client does not want any seller or prospective seller to know that the hirer is acting as his agent. Your present task is to draft a clause to that effect.

Legal subject and legal action   Your first draft might read:

> The Hirer shall not disclose to any Seller or to any third party that the Hirer is the agent of the Lessor.

The legal subject is 'The Hirer' and the legal action is 'shall not disclose to any Seller or to any third party that the Hirer is the agent of the Lessor' (a negative mandatory legal action).

The case   Although clearly implied, the other party may insist that this undertaking be restricted so that it operates only in relation to third parties with whom he deals as potential sellers in connection with a purchase contract. Your second draft might then read:

> Where, in the course of dealing in connection with a Purchase Contract, the Hirer (legal subject), shall not disclose to any Seller or to any third party that the Hirer is the agent of the Lessor (legal action).

The words 'Where in the course of dealing in connection with a Purchase Contract' constitute the case, the circumstances in which the rule is to operate. Note the use of the word 'where'. This is the usual to way to introduce the case in a legal sentence. Sometimes, usually where time periods are involved, the case begins 'When'. Another form introduces the case with the word 'if' and resumes the sentence with the word 'then'.

The condition   Your client may have conceded in negotiations that there may be occasions when there could be no objection to the hirer disclosing the identity of the principal. When you accommodate this point in your draft you will want to ensure that, where the hirer wishes to name your client as principal, your client has the opportunity of assessing whether it would be appropriate. There are two possible approaches. The first is:

> Where, in the course of dealing in connection with a Purchase Contract (case), unless the Lessor has given written consent (condition), the Hirer (legal subject) shall not disclose to any Seller or to any third party that the Hirer is the agent of the Lessor (legal action).

The phrase 'unless the Lessor has given written consent' provides what Coode described as the *condition* in a sentence. This example uses a negative condition. A positive condition begins with 'If the Lessor has given written consent (condition)' and continues, 'the Hirer may disclose . . .'.

Alternatively, you could define the legal subject more closely:

> In the course of dealing in connection with a Purchase Contract (case), a Hirer, who has not obtained the Lessor's written consent to do so (legal subject), shall not disclose to any Seller or to any third party that the Hirer is the agent of the Lessor (legal action).

The expression 'legal sentence' should not be taken too literally. In many clauses, as with the example above, it may be possible to state the case, condition, legal subject and legal action all in one sentence. In a lengthy clause with many qualifications and exceptions it may still be possible to keep to the continuous sentence, breaking it up by 'paragraphing' and display. Alternatively, it may be more convenient to arrange the clause in subclauses each of which consist of a complete sentence. Whichever method you choose, one sentence or several, you should follow Coode's logic and order of arrangement.

3.14.2.3 Shall and will

In the examples given above, the word 'shall' is not used except in the legal action. 'Shall' should never be used in a case or a condition. Coode remarked that the use of 'shall' in stating the case or condition 'confounds the proper language of obligation with that of hypothesis'. Unfortunately, examples such as those illustrated below are very common:

If execution shall be levied against the borrower....

If the Purchaser shall fail to pay....

If the company shall go into liquidation....

If it shall appear to a court....

If the lender shall have given notice to the borrower....

Where any person shall find himself aggrieved....

Draftsmen often use 'shall' in this way through a desire to state a case or condition in the future tense. Its use is, however, based on a confusion between the words 'shall' and 'will'. These two verbs complement each other. You should adopt a systematic distinction between them.

'Shall' should be used in the first person to express simple futurity:

I shall have your document ready for signature by Friday morning,

and in the second and third person to express obligations or determinations:

The Tenant shall keep the premises in good repair.

You shall have your day in court.

'Will' should be used to express simple futurity in the second and third person:

You will have my document ready for signature by Friday morning,

and to express obligations or determinations in the first person:

I will keep and maintain. . . .

'Shall' should be confined to describing a legal action and not used in a
case or condition. Use it only to indicate that there is a legal obligation
and not to represent the future. In legal documents (as in English
generally) the present, present perfect or past tense is appropriate in a
'where', 'if' or 'unless' clause. In most cases it is implied that the
agreement is to be treated as 'continuously present'.

The following are the correct forms for the examples given above:

If execution is levied against the borrower. . . .

If the Purchaser fails to pay. . . .

If the company goes into liquidation. . . .

If it appears to a court. . . .

If the lender has given notice to the borrower. . . .

Where any person finds himself aggrieved. . . .

If you are in any doubt use a phrase such as:

If at any time. . . .

Where you feel it necessary to use the future tense 'will' and not 'shall'
should be used (except in the rare case where a document is drafted in
the first person).

For example, a covenant to manufacture goods might be expressed as:

The Seller shall manufacture the goods in accordance with the
specifications set out in Schedule 1 to this agreement.

Whereas a warranty that the goods will comply with a certain description
might be expressed as:

The Seller warrants that the goods will be manufactured in accordance
with the specifications set out in Schedule 1 to this agreement.

3.14.2.4 'Shall', 'may' and 'is'

Sometimes 'shall' is inappropriate, even where it is used in the legal action. The word 'may' or the simple present tense may be what is required.

The present tense, 'is' or 'are' ('includes', 'means' etc.), and not 'shall', is appropriate in definition clauses and other provisions which simply state agreed facts or contractual rules. In these instances 'shall' is unnecessary because there is no need to impose an obligation on a legal subject. For example:

A 'time of day' is, unless otherwise stated, a reference to London time.

The dollar is the currency of account and payment under this Agreement.

This Agreement is governed by and shall be construed in accordance with the law of England.

In the last example, whilst there is no need for 'shall' in 'This Agreement is governed by', its inclusion in 'and shall be construed in accordance with the law of England' can be justified on the ground that it imposes an obligation on persons construing the document to construe it in accordance with English law.

Where you intend to create a permission or a discretion rather than an obligation, the legal action should be permissive rather than mandatory. Here the word 'may' is preferred over such phrases as 'it shall be lawful' or 'shall be at liberty to' which clumsily combine the command of 'shall' with a verbose permissive expression:

Upon signature of this Agreement, the Customer shall pay a deposit. (Mandatory.)

If the Customer fails to collect the goods on or before the Delivery date the Company may retain the deposit. (Permissive.)

Once again, use 'may' only to denote that a permission is given, not to indicate the future.

3.14.3   Use of provisos

It is sometimes necessary, having provided a general rule, to state that it does not apply in certain cases. Draftsmen often do this by the use of a device known as a 'proviso'. It is introduced by such phrases as 'provided that' or 'provided always that'. Frequently, these expressions appear in block capitals to signal that a provision is subject to a proviso.

Provisos are seldom used correctly and are very rarely necessary. In practice provisos are often used by draftsmen as an afterthought. At the end of a sentence they find that they have omitted something from a case, condition or subject and seek to remedy the omission by adding a spurious proviso.

Coode disliked the proviso, describing it as 'that bane of all correct composition'. In his view, most exceptions or qualifications could best be stated within the structure of the legal sentence rather than as a proviso at the end. He particularly disapproved of the tendency of some draftsmen to use a spurious proviso wherever the application of a general rule needed to be modified or restricted. He wrote:

> the present use of the proviso by the best draftsman is very anomalous. It is often used to introduce mere exceptions to the operation of an enactment where no special provision is made for such exceptions. But it is obvious that such exceptions would be better expressed as exceptions; if particular cases were excepted, to be expressed in the case; if particular conditions were dispensed with, to be expressed in the condition; if certain persons were to be excluded from the operation of the enactment, to be expressed in the subject. In fact, where the enunciation of the general provision is merely to be negatived in some particular, the proper place for the expression of that negation is by an exception expressed in immediate contact with the general words by which the particular would otherwise be included. This would make, in all cases the definition of the case, condition, subject, or action, complete at once, that is to say, it would show in immediate contact all that is included and all that is excluded.

3.14.3.1   'True' and 'traditional' provisos
The true proviso states a special rule for special circumstances. The correctly used proviso states a special case followed immediately by a

special rule to fit that case. Therefore, a provision containing a true proviso will usually begin with 'where' or 'if'.

In some documents it is traditional to use provisos and you should adopt the accepted form. Examples are the proviso for redemption in mortgages and the proviso for re-entry in leases. Otherwise, unless you are confident that you are using a proviso correctly, it is generally best to avoid them. This has the added advantage that you avoid the special rules of construction that apply to the interpretation of provisos.

3.14.3.2 Exceptions
You can avoid the use of spurious provisos by distributing the exceptions or qualifications among other parts of the sentence, such as the case or legal subject though, where an exception affects a clause as a whole, it is usually best to state it at the beginning of the sentence.

Where you opt for the first approach and alter the case, condition or subject, avoid using the inelegant and ungrammatical expression 'provided that'. It is usually possible simply to substitute 'but'. For example:

> Where, in the course of dealing in connection with a Purchase Contract, unless the Lessor has given written consent, the Hirer shall not disclose to any Seller or to any third party that the Hirer is the agent of the Lessor PROVIDED THAT the Hirer may disclose that it is acting as agent for an undisclosed principal.

> Where, in the course of dealing in connection with a Purchase Contract, unless the Lessor has given written consent, the Hirer shall not disclose to any Seller or to any third party that the Hirer is the agent of the Lessor but the Hirer may disclose that it is acting as agent for an undisclosed principal.

Where you use the 'opening exception' approach you may find that reciting the full exception may involve adding undue length to the sentence. In such cases, you can state the exception in a second, self-contained, subclause and incorporate it in your sentence by cross-reference. The first subclause being expressed to be subject to the second. For example:

Except as provided in subclause 5.4 below....

Subject to the restriction in Article 6....

Subject to subclause (C) of this clause....

3.15   CHOICE OF WORDS

When drafting documents, you should not lose sight of the general principles of legal writing set out in chapter 1. You should try to use short, simple, familiar words, keep technical words and jargon to a minimum and avoid foreign phrases and redundant expressions.

In particular you should avoid archaic and redundant legal expressions, negatives and the passive voice. This section returns to apply these general principles in the context of drafting. Consistency, the golden rule of drafting, is also revisited.

3.15.1   Redundant legal expressions

The traditional and unthinking use of 'legal pairs', where two words, or sometimes three, are used to express the same thing in a variety of ways, was criticised in 1.7.4.4. The time for exorcising these ancient ghosts is long overdue. If you learn to draft in simple modern English your clients will thank you for it.

'Null and void', 'suffer or permit' and 'last will and testament' were given as examples of redundant pairs in 1.7.4.4. Here are some more:

In the expression, 'Lands, tenements and hereditaments', 'tenements' is obsolete and 'hereditaments' refers to property which passes to an heir. In most cases 'land' will suffice.

In old forms, you may see that a party 'covenants and agrees'. It is quite sufficient to use either word alone although, strictly, 'covenant' should be used only in a deed. You may also see a party's obligations under the agreement described in a provision as 'covenants, conditions, agreements or stipulations' when any one of these would usually be enough. Indeed, the word 'obligations' may be an adequate substitute. In a deed the noun 'covenant' will normally cover all the obligations. The older form of covenant may contain such expressions as 'shall and will' or 'shall not nor will'. A modern document needs only 'shall' or 'shall not'.

A provision frequently found in a lease requires the tenant to 'well and sufficiently repair, uphold, maintain'. It is doubtful whether the additional words add anything to the meaning of the word 'repair' (see *Anstruther-Gough-Calthorpe* v *McOscar* [1924] 1 KB 716).

In most cases there is no useful distinction to be drawn between the two words in 'pay and discharge' or the four words in 'bear, pay, satisfy and discharge'. They can usually be reduced to a simple 'pay'. Similarly there can rarely be any merit in using the formula 'due and payable'.

The intricate and archaic language of 'by and in the said deed of settlement declared and contained' can be replaced by the plain 'contained in the settlement'. 'Fall into and become part of my residual estate' can be reduced by selecting either 'fall into' or 'become part of'.

There are many, many more examples of redundant pairs and triplets to be found in the precedent books that are ripe for similar treatment. When you come across a precedent which contains a word-wasting pair consider whether it would be better to find a single apt word or phrase. Sometimes it may be necessary to give the term you choose a definition for the avoidance of doubt or to modify its ordinary meaning but you can then use it in isolation without surrounding it with the words you have now defined it to include.

However, exercise caution. Not all legal expressions that appear to involve pairs can be reduced to a single word. Where more than one word is used and they are not synonyms, one word may be intended to modify the other or to provide a wider definition than the one word standing alone. For example, the word 'sale', in the absence of specific legislative provision or clear evidence of a contrary intention, means an exchange of property for cash and not for other property. So that the expression 'sell, transfer or dispose' in pre-emption rights should not be reduced to a simple 'sell'. Checking your ground in the law library and discussing it with other more experienced lawyers will take time, but to test an ill-considered new phrase in the law courts would be an expensive and possibly disastrous experiment at the client's expense.

3.15.2 Archaic language

In 1.7.5 it was suggested that lawyers' archaic phrases rarely add anything of significance and are often used quite needlessly. The claim that these expressions are somehow more precise than ordinary modern English does not withstand close examination. Words such as 'said', 'hereinbefore', and similar referential phrases are usually inserted as a matter of habit and when removed or replaced with modern equivalents their true worth (or lack of it) is exposed. These expressions create a false impression of precision when in reality they may conceal lazy thinking.

3.15.2.1 'Herein', 'hereof', 'hereunder', 'hereinbefore' and 'hereinafter'

There is a common belief that when making a reference to another clause of the same agreement the drafter should always qualify the cross-reference by one of these words to make it clear that the clause referred to by number is a clause of the same agreement. The context usually makes this clear but if you feel it is appropriate to qualify cross-references in this way, use the modern terms, 'above' or 'below'.

Sometimes the use of 'herein', 'hereof' or 'hereunder' can cause ambiguity. It may not be clear whether the 'here-word' means 'in this document' or 'in this present clause'. It is better to spell out precisely what you mean. For example, with a subclause that starts with the phrase:

Subject to the provisions hereof,

it may be impossible to say whether it takes effect subject only to other provisions of that clause or to all provisions in the agreement. You should therefore refer specifically to the provision to which the subclause is subject:

Subject to the provisions of subparagraph 7(B)(ii)(c).

Subject to the provisions of this clause.

Subject to the provisions of this agreement.

Being as specific as possible assists the reader who will know whether or not it is necessary to search the whole document for all possible references. Further, if you are specific you will reduce the chance of including an unintended reference. For example, if you say 'subject to the provisions of this agreement' when you contemplate clauses 5 and 6 being relevant, but you have overlooked the possibility of clause 11 also being considered relevant or applicable, then you may find that your lack of precision brings about unintended results.

The old method of signifying an abbreviation by the formula 'hereinafter referred to as' is better replaced with the modern practice of using brackets and quotation marks to contain the abbreviation.

3.15.2.2 'Hereby' and 'hereby agrees with'

You should avoid using 'hereby' in phrases such as 'hereby give notice' where it merely dresses up a simple message with mock ceremony. The word is almost always superfluous and can be deleted without loss of meaning.

For the same reason there is rarely any need to commence a provision with 'X hereby agrees with Y' or 'X hereby covenants with Y', since the operative part of the agreement or deed will usually be introduced by: 'IT IS HEREBY AGREED as follows:'. In any event, the fact that a document stating that a person shall do something has been signed by that person is enough to impose a legal obligation to do that thing without any express statement that the person agrees to do it (see *Dawes* v *Tredwell* (1881) 18 ChD 354 at p. 359). However, it may be necessary to use such a formulation in a provision where:

(a) There are three or more parties to an agreement and it is necessary to establish by whom particular obligations may be enforced; for example, can X's promise be enforced by only some of the other parties or by each of them?

(b) Two or more persons make the same undertaking and it is necessary to make it clear whether they do so jointly, or jointly and severally, or severally.

3.15.2.3 'Do', 'doth', 'hath' etc.

Probably the most antiquated words still found in some precedents (although now relatively infrequently) are the archaic forms of verbs which end in 'th' for the third person singular present tense, for example, 'hath agreed', and the redundant use of 'do', as in 'do hereby grant' or 'doth hereby give notice'. These expressions should be brought up to date as 'have agreed', 'grant', 'gives notice' (note the deletion of 'hereby').

A more common practice is the continued use of the word 'witnesseth' in deeds. For example, where a formula is used to introduce the operative provisions:

NOW THIS DEED WITNESSETH as follows

There is no reason why the more modern 'witnesses' should not be preferred. Similarly, 'situate', as in 'the property situate at' should be modernised as 'situated'.

3.15.2.4 'Said' and its relations

Of all the antique words and expressions used by lawyers, probably the most objectionable is the expression 'the said' and its synonym 'the aforesaid'. Unfortunately many lawyers have developed a compulsion for prefacing a repeated name or description with an automatic 'said' or 'aforesaid'. Unless a clear contrary intention appears, it would be perverse to suggest that, where a person or article is referred to in a document by name or description, a subsequent mention of that name, unqualified by 'said' or 'aforesaid', will be understood as referring to some other article or person.

It is true that, where other persons or articles have been mentioned, a general expression such as 'the ship' may need to be distinguished from other ships. But simply referring to 'the said ship' is, at best, a very cumbersome method. Further, it is often of no help at all because, if another ship has been mentioned by name, that ship could also qualify as 'the said ship'. Some lawyers will respond that, in such a case, common sense will dictate that the repeated contexts in which the expression 'the said ship' has been used leads to the inescapable conclusion that the expression can only refer to 'the first-mentioned ship'. But if this is so why not dispense with 'said' altogether? The same logic applies with or without it. Sadly, some of those who habitually rely on 'said' may be so shaken by this argument that they might be tempted to start using 'the first-mentioned' instead.

One lawyer, in an attempt to refute this argument, recently advanced the example of the expression 'my wife' used in a will. He said that failure to use 'my said wife' in later references risked the possibility of unintentionally benefiting a party to a later marriage. Leaving aside the likelihood that a subsequent marriage would revoke the will, he had missed the point. The addition of the word 'said' cannot cure an inherently ambiguous expression. The correct approach is to be specific from the outset. For example, 'my wife Mary Jane Edwards' used throughout. To add 'said' to this phrase (as you will sometimes see in practice) is as superfluous as it is ridiculous.

It is absurd to purport to distinguish a person or thing from another when there is no real risk of confusion. Yet lawyers regularly do so. I recently saw an extreme example of this where 'said' had been applied to a date (which by definition is unique). What the drafter was thinking as he wrote 'the said 5 May 1992' is a mystery. What seems certain is that he was not thinking about the function and the meaning of the word 'said'.

If 'said' is being used as merely a way to avoid pointless repetition, for example, on first mention 'the ship, *HMS Lollipop*' and from there onwards 'the said ship', this is more acceptable. But the more modern device of stating the full name followed by a 'nickname' which is used from then on (see 3.12.2) does away with the need for 'said' altogether, for example, '*HMS Lollipop* (the Ship)'.

3.15.2.5 *'The same'*
The 'same' is a lawyer's clumsy attempt at elegant variation (see 1.10.4.2).

When you are tempted to write 'the same', consider first whether a pronoun like 'it' or 'them' could be used instead without causing ambiguity. Otherwise an abbreviation or 'nickname' will usually provide the answer. It is, however, conceded that the device 'and the same applies in relation to' (although it contains two undesirable expressions) can be extremely useful to avoid needless repetition.

3.15.2.6 *'Such'*
The correct meaning of 'such' is 'of that type' and it is followed by 'a' or 'as'. For example, the use of 'such' in subclause (a) below is correct whereas subclause (b) uses 'such' in a similar manner to the way in which 'said' is used.

The Purchaser shall:

(a)   pay *such* taxes or charges *as* are mentioned in this Agreement; and

(b)   indemnify the Vendor against any liability which it may incur for *such a* tax or charge.

When 'such' is used in a similar way to the archaic 'said', to refer to a previous noun, much the same objections apply. Many lawyers have acquired the 'such habit': if a provision refers to an item more than once, they feel compelled to put 'such' before each subsequent reference.

Here is an example taken from an equipment lease in use in the mid 1980s. In addition to other ailments, this subclause has no fewer than 11 'such's. Only the last is justified.

In the event that capital allowances in respect of the Goods in an amount equal to 100 per cent of the Total Cost shall not be available to the Lessor for the Accounting Period in which *such* expenditure is incurred or that *such* capital allowances shall be withdrawn for *such* period but *such* capital allowances become available to the Lessor in respect of *such* Goods at a later time or times the Lessor shall be under no obligation to apply for, utilise or give credit for any *such* allowances PROVIDED THAT if the Lessor actually utilises any *such* allowances and obtains the benefit therefrom, the Lessor shall take into account *such* utilisation and benefit and shall adjust each *such* instalment of Primary Period Rent payable after receipt of *such* benefit in *such* manner as the Lessor in its sole discretion considers appropriate.

'Such' is usually unnecessary and 'the', 'that', 'those', 'they' or 'them' can be used without loss of meaning. 'Such' is always unnecessary if it accompanies a defined term.

More seriously, 'such', when used like 'said', can cause ambiguity. The reader may not realise that 'such' is being used in this way and continue to look for a correlative 'as' or, alternatively, may not be certain which of several nouns the 'such' refers to or be unclear whether phrases qualifying the noun are also intended to apply.

In *Mountifield* v *Ward* [1897] 1 QB 326, a case concerning the Licensing Act 1874 (since repealed), the Divisional Court had to construe the following provision:

> Nothing in this Act or in the principal Act contained shall preclude a person licensed to sell any intoxicating liquor to be consumed on the premises from selling such liquor at any time to bona fide travellers.

The question for the court was whether the section permitted the sale of liquor for consumption off the premises or the sale of intoxicating liquor to bona fide travellers at any time but only if it was to be consumed on the premises. The majority view was that the words 'such liquor' referred both to 'intoxicating liquor' and to 'intoxicating liquor to be consumed on the premises'.

The moral is, wherever possible avoid use of 'such'. Where you do use this word be aware of the dangers and guard against them.

3.15.2.7 *'Whatsoever', 'whosoever' and 'wheresoever'*

Words such as 'whatsoever', 'whosoever' and 'wheresoever' are examples of overused modifying words invented by lawyers to create special emphasis or to ensure that every eventuality is covered. They are often quite unnecessary, as in the embarrassingly tautologous, 'totally null and void and of no effect whatsoever'. Where a qualifying word of this kind is necessary, it can usually be improved by dropping the '-so-'. Otherwise, the use of the simple 'any' will often do the job of 'whatsoever' quite satisfactorily.

3.15.3   Avoiding negatives (and double negatives)

Avoid negatives and double negatives (see 1.5.4). The use of a positive phrase is usually preferable to a negative because it is more direct and usually shorter. More seriously, negatives can accumulate to require your readers to perform mental somersaults and render your drafting prone to error.

The need to avoid cumulative negatives is critical in drafting because provisions commonly require qualifications and exceptions. Wherever possible, you should state general principles as positive statements. If they are stated as a double negative, exceptions will normally add a third negative and qualifications to those exceptions may require a fourth. If further exceptions and restrictions become necessary, as they often do, following negotiations based on the draft, your drafting will be very difficult to read and understand. Worse, the cumulative negatives will not only make it easier for you to make the sort of mistakes illustrated at 1.5.4 but also make it more difficult for you and others to spot them.

3.15.4 Active voice

The use of verbs and, in particular, the active and passive voice, is dealt with in detail in 1.8. As with other forms of writing, it is generally preferable to draft in the active voice and you should avoid using the passive unless there is good reason for doing so.

The most serious objection to the use of the passive voice in drafting is its potential for ambiguity. When using passive verbs it is possible to write sentences that omit the identity of the agent or (in terms of Coode's rule) the legal subject. A sentence truncated in this way may withhold vital information. This will often happen if the passive is used in sentences which contemplate someone taking some form of action. Where a sentence is expressed in truncated passive form, the agent or the legal subject is disclosed only by implication. For example:

The leased premises shall be maintained in good repair.

Notice shall be given. . . .

Nothing shall be done to the annoyance or inconvenience of the Landlord.

With the first obligation, the lease does not specify who is to keep the premises in good repair and the second provision does not make it clear who is to give notice. In each case is it the landlord or tenant? The uncertainty in the third obligation is wider in scope. What would be the position if inconvenience or annoyance were caused to the landlord by the action of third parties? The ambiguity may be resolved against the landlord seeking to terminate the tenancy on grounds of alleged breach even where the tenant permitted or neglected to prevent the actions of the third party.

You can ensure that you have identified the agent in a sentence if you make the legal subject of your sentence a legal person as opposed to an inanimate object or other receiver of the action:

The Tenant shall maintain the leased premises in good repair.

The Tenant shall give notice. . . .

The Tenant shall not do or suffer to be done anything to the annoyance or inconvenience of the Landlord.

3.15.5 Repetition

3.15.5.1 Slight variance
You should exercise great care when repeating phrases. You can cause dangerous confusion if you fail to use exactly the same words. The variance may be interpreted as intentional and the words construed differently. For example, problems can occur where a phrase is used first in a recital and again in the operative part of an agreement. In their different contexts they may produce two distinct results (see below) or, where the context does not permit this conclusion, the operative part will prevail over the recital, producing potential unintended results.

The golden rule of legal writing and drafting is: be consistent. This dictates that you should:

(a) Never change your language unless you intend to signal a change in meaning.

(b) Always change your language where you intend to signal a change in meaning.

3.15.5.2 Use of synonyms
Elegant variation is particularly inappropriate in legal drafting. The reader of a legal document is entitled to assume that, in general, a change of words is intended to signify a change in meaning. A common example of confusion caused by bad practice is a provision which, dealing with calculations and payments, alternates between 'sum' and 'amount' to refer to the same item. In an agreement or other formal document the avoidance of repetition by use of synonyms is not only undesirable, it can

be dangerous. For example, the use of 'liabilities' as a synonym for 'debts' may result in the word 'debts' being interpreted as excluding contingent liabilities, e.g. under a guarantee (see *Re Pinto Leite, ex parte Visconde Des Olivaes & Nephews* [1929] 1 Ch 221 at p. 235; *Marren v Ingles* [1980] 1 WLR 983 at p. 990, HL).

A residential lease, used by a substantial estate agent, unforgivably oscillates between 'the Tenant' and 'the lessee' causing the prospective lessee/tenant to wonder whether he is one or other or both of these and, if so, what the difference is. The same lease contains the following clause (without punctuation):

> ANY notice to be given hereunder shall be deemed to be properly given if sent by Registered Post or First Class Recorded Delivery addressed if given to the Landlord to him by name at Val Hewitt & Floggit, Lemon Street, Suburbiton, IT5 5AD and if given to the Tenant to him by name at the address of the Premises and if so sent shall be deemed to have been served not later than the first working day following the day on which it was posted.

At first sight, the use of the word 'served' might appear to mean something other than 'given', but the provisions referring to notices in the lease only refer to notices being 'given'. The tenant is left to ponder the extra significance of the word 'served'. The unfortunate use of 'if given' to indicate the person to whom notice is 'to be given' seems to beg the question.

The clause is probably intended to specify exclusively the methods of giving notice. Its effect, however, is simply to deem certain methods as proper notice while leaving the possibility of other methods of giving notice open. In an earlier clause the tenant undertakes to 'give immediate notice' of 'any damage or destruction or loss happening to the premises or the contents'. One amusing (and presumably unintentional) side-effect of the notice provision is that if the tenant gives notice of damage by first class post to the estate agents, it will deem him or her to have given 'immediate' notice.

3.15.5.3 Tabulation
For example, in the following extract from an equipment lease, tabulation has been used to avoid starting several sentences with the words 'The Lessee shall insure and maintain insurance'.

The Lessee shall at its own cost insure and maintain insurance:

(a)   of the goods to a value of not less than the full replacement cost;

(b)   for such amount as is consistent with a high degree of prudence in all the circumstances to cover any legal liability which may be incurred by the Lessor................................; and

(c)   against such other or further risks as may be required by statute, regulation or order...

3.15.5.4   *Use of pronouns*

Where the repeated word is a noun, a pronoun may often take its place to improve the flow of the passage, e.g., 'he'; 'she'; 'him'; 'her'; 'it'; 'each'; 'either'. If you can replace a noun with a pronoun with no loss of clarity, repetition of the noun is pedantic and should be avoided.

The person who drafted the following confidential information clause, extracted from an employment contract, allowed himself (or herself) only one pronoun used twice ('his' for 'the employee's').

5.   Confidential Information

The employee shall not, except as authorised by the employer or required by the employee's duties under the employee's contract of employment, use for his own benefit or gain or divulge to any persons, firm, company or other organisation any confidential information belonging to the employer or relating to the employer's affairs or dealings which may come to the employee's knowledge during his employment.

This approach is over cautious and the result seems cumbersome but it is easy to see how greater use of 'his' might risk confusion in a contract of employment, particularly if used for 'employer' as well as 'employee'. However, the use of the pronoun 'you', in addition to creating a more human and personal (and non-sexist) tone, removes the necessity for repeated use of 'employee' and enables the use of another pronoun as a substitute for 'employer'.

5.   Confidential Information

You shall not, except as authorised by the employer or required by your duties under your contract of employment, use for your own benefit or gain or divulge to any persons, firm, company or other organisation any confidential information belonging to the employer or relating to his affairs or dealings which may come to your knowledge during your employment.

However, careless use of 'you' can produce unintended results. The following extract from a law firm's staff handbook was intended to introduce a restriction on staff claims for reimbursement for taxi fares following late night working. No doubt 'you' was used in an attempt to give the handbook a human face. Failure to use it consistently produced this bizarre provision.

LATE NIGHT WORKING
If support staff are required to work after 8.00 pm, you may arrange at the firm's expense a taxi to your home (within greater London) or to an appropriate London British Rail terminus (if you live outside greater London).

The draftsman intended to extend the entitlement to support staff only. Read literally, not only does it appear to extend the entitlement to all staff ('you'), it seems to do so whenever a member of support staff is required to work after 8.00 pm and, when this condition is satisfied, all staff may claim irrespective of the time of their travel.

Use pronouns but be careful. If you are in any doubt, repeat the noun. Always prefer certainty over elegance.

3.15.5.5   *Abbreviations and defined words*
The repetition of lengthy phrases can be relieved by the use of abbreviations and definitions. By giving a short name to a long phrase you can avoid wholesale repetition. This has the added advantage of avoiding the use of 'the said' or 'the same'.

3.16   FINAL CONSIDERATIONS

3.16.1   Precautions and procedures

3.16.1.1   *Identifying drafts*
It is good practice to mark the front sheet (if there is one) and the first page of a draft document with the words 'draft', the number of that draft,

the date the draft was prepared and the reference which identifies the partner, assistant solicitor and, where appropriate, the trainee who produced the draft and the word processing file, directory or system in which it was produced.

Failure to identify documents can waste time by making the search for the document unnecessarily difficult and, in some circumstances (for example, where you are taken ill or otherwise away from the office unexpectedly) making it necessary to retype the document. It can also cause mayhem when it becomes necessary to re-trace steps in the 'chain of drafts' in a transaction. Failure to date or number a draft can result in an old, rather than the latest, draft being marked-up for amendment with potentially disastrous consequences.

3.16.1.2   Keeping previous drafts
Keep all previous drafts of a document in a file, in the order they were produced, making sure that the pages of each draft are securely held together with staples (not sliding paper-clips). Keep the current draft in a separate part of the file (perhaps in a plastic wallet) marked 'current draft' in coloured ink. When it has been superseded strike out these words and place the document in the file with the previous drafts.

3.16.1.3   Identifying blanks
You can reduce the risk of executing an incomplete document by placing all blanks or optional text in square brackets rather than leaving them as blank spaces. This provides a marker for your eye to locate all the places in the document where some further input is required. This task has been made easier in recent years since most word-processors are capable of finding, for example, all opening square brackets.

3.16.1.4   Definitions checklist
If you have followed the suggestion at the beginning of 3.6, you will have prepared a definitions checklist which you will have modified as you produced your draft. Now you have completed your draft you should note each occasion a defined term is used and mark it with a colour or highlighting pen. This will help when you check that the relevant definitions fit the context.

3.16.1.5   Cross-references
It will aid the checking process if you mark all cross-references with a colour or highlighting pen.

3.16.1.6 'Sleep on it'

Before you check a document, it pays to 'sleep on it'. If time permits, once you have completed your draft, do not launch straight into proofreading. Leave your draft to one side overnight, over lunch or even while you deal with your post or telephone messages. Give your mind a break, come back to it afresh and be critical.

3.16.2   Checking the draft

As the author of the document it is your responsibility to check it for errors and omissions. In a document prepared by a solicitor even minor typographical errors are unacceptable. The most expertly drafted document will not impress your client or gain the respect of your colleagues if it contains such errors.

Beware in particular:

Figures, dates and names   It is very easy to skip over these seemingly mundane matters but an error is an error and the wrong figure, date or name can have disastrous consequences.

Punctuation   You should check punctuation marks as carefully as the words themselves. In particular, check commas and brackets to ensure that where there is a commencing comma (used in parenthesis) or bracket there is a closing one in the appropriate place.

Common 'typos'   Keep your eyes open for common typographical errors. A particularly deadly confusion is the one between 'not' and 'now'. An error of this kind can reverse the intended meaning of the sentence. This mistake, notorious in the days when shorthand was widely used because of the similarity of symbols, is fortunately less common in modern times.

Today, a poor technique when using a dictating machine may result in an array of potentially disastrous errors. Many of these will be the result of your own idiosyncrasies. So talk to your secretary about the quality of your dictation, make a note of frequently misheard and mistyped words and look out for them in future documents. 'And' and 'or' are often confused. In *Re Horrocks* [1939] P 198, a typewritten will read, 'charitable *or* benevolent object or objects'. It was alleged that the solicitor had dictated 'charitable *and* benevolent '. Unfortunately for the solicitor and his clients, the court held the evidence of the error to be insufficient and the trust failed for uncertainty.

Handwriting also has its idiosyncrasies. For example, in a handwritten draft it is possible for 'any' to be read as 'my'. In *Re Harpur* [1940] ALR 178, an Australian case, a will was drafted to read 'after the death of *any* son' but when it was engrossed it read 'after the death of *my* son'.

Re-numbering and cross-references   The classic error in drafting is to cross-refer to the wrong provision or to one that no longer exists. As a document goes through a number of drafts it is highly likely that original numbering and lettering of clauses, subclauses, and other subdivisions will be altered. Take great care to check that all cross-references have been updated.

Defined words   Check that you have given definitions to all words and expressions capable of material ambiguity. Check also that you have applied your definitions consistently and that each time a defined term is used the definition fits the context and produces the desired result.

Other consequential amendments   Beware of inconsistencies between provisions and do not neglect any part of your document in the checking process. For example, recitals describing the transaction are frequently forgotten after the first draft. The transaction may be modified during negotiations in such a way that a conflict between an operative provision and a recital arises.

Another example of consequential errors is where marginal notes or sub-headings are used in an incomplete draft but overlooked when the document is amended and checked. The use of marginal notes and subheadings is generally undesirable. If they are used it may be appropriate to include a provision in the interpretation clause making it clear that the headings and marginal notes are for ease of reference and are not to be used in the interpretation of the document.

Appendix

Undesirables Checklist

Expression	Objection	Preferred options
'a cut above'	cliché	DELETE
ab extra	foreign	'from outside'
'absolutely'; 'absolutely [unique]'	over-used qualifying word / tautology qualification of an absolute	DELETE
'acid test'	cliché	DELETE
[by this] 'act and deed'	legal pair	select one word and use it consistently
'actual'	vogue word	DELETE
'ad verbum'	foreign	'verbally'
'agrees and declares' or 'acknowledges and agrees'	redundant words	DELETE – 'will' or shall' invariably suffice – the introduction or nature of the document makes clear it is an agreement
'all and singular'	legal pair	'all'
'alter or change'	legal pair	select one word and use it consistently
'amazing'	vogue word	DELETE
'any matter, fact or thing'	redundant words	'anything'

Expression	*Objection*	*Preferred options*
'ascend up'	tautology	select one word and use it consistently
'astronomical'	vogue word	DELETE
'at a later date'	redundant words	'later'
'at that point in time'	compound	'at that time' or 'then'
'at this point in time'	compound	'now'
'at your earliest convenience'	cliché antique formula	'soon' or 'as soon as [you can] [practicable] [possible]'
'awful'	vogue word	DELETE
'background'	over-used metaphor	avoid
'basis'	abstract	rephrase using more specific words
'beg to advise'	clichéd antique expression	DELETE
'bequeath'	archaic	'give'
'bitter irony'	cliché	DELETE
'blend together'	tautology	select one word and use it consistently
'blueprint'	over-used metaphor	avoid
'bottleneck'	over-used metaphor	avoid
'breakdown	over-used metaphor	avoid
'by means of'	compound	'by'
'by reason of'	compound	'because of'
'by virtue of'	compound	'by' or 'under'
'cards on the table'	cliché	DELETE
'catalyst'	over-used metaphor	avoid
'cease'	unfamiliar	'stop' or 'end'
'cease and desist'	legal pair	select one word and use it consistently
'ceiling'	over-used metaphor	avoid
'ceteris paribus'	foreign	other things being equal
'circa'	foreign	'about'
'circumstances'	abstract	rephrase using more specific words
'clearly' 'clear beyond dispute'	redundant	DELETE
'cohort'	vogue word	DELETE

Expression	*Objection*	*Preferred options*
'commencement'	unfamiliar	'beginning'
'completely'; 'completely [convinced; finished]'	over-used qualifying word/tautology qualification of an absolute	DELETE
'concept'; 'conceptual'	vogue/abstract word	rephrase using more specific words
'condense down'	tautology	select one word and use it consistently
'confessed and acknowledged'	legal pair	select one word and use it consistently
'contents duly noted'	clichéd antique formula	DELETE
'context'	vogue word	DELETE
'continue on'	tautology	select one word and use it consistently
'convey, transfer and set over'	legal triplet	select one word and use it consistently
'cooperate together'	tautology	select one word and use it consistently
coup de grâce	foreign	'final stroke'
'covenants and agrees'	legal pair	DELETE or use 'will', 'shall' or 'covenants'
'dark horse'	cliché	DELETE
'demise'	unfamiliar	'lease'
'is desirous of'	clichéd antique formula	'wishes to'
'devise'	archaic	'give'
'diabolical'	vogue word	DELETE
'dispatch'	unfamiliar	'send'
'doth'	archaic	DELETE – e.g. change 'X doth hereby mortgage' to 'X mortgages'
'dreadful'	vogue word	DELETE
'donate'	unfamiliar	'give'
'do and perform'	legal pair	select one word and use it consistently

Expression	Objection	Preferred options
'duly'	redundant word	means 'fitly, properly or punctually' and is often unnecessary or inapt
'during such time as'	compound	'while'
'each and every'	legal pair	'each', 'any' or 'all' (depending on context)
'elements'	abstract	rephrase using more specific words
'elucidate'	unfamiliar	'explain'
'endeavour'	unfamiliar	'try'
'*en masse*'	foreign	'in a body', 'as a whole'
'*eo instante*'	foreign	'instantly', 'automatically', 'at the same time'
'ergo'	foreign	'therefore'
'even date'	archaic	'of the same date'
'*ex post facto*'	foreign	'after the event', 'retrospectively'
'expedite'; 'expeditious'	unfamiliar	'hurry' or 'hasten'; 'speedy' or 'quick'
'expressly' (when used as in, 'the Borrower hereby expressly agrees')	redundant	DELETE ALWAYS (in this context it is always tautologous)
'far and away'	cliché	DELETE
'fabulous'	vogue word	DELETE
'facet'	abstract	rephrase using more specific words
'fact': e.g. 'in fact'; 'the fact that'; 'plus the fact that'; 'please note the fact that'; 'despite the fact that'	redundant	DELETE
'factor'	abstract	rephrase using more specific words
'fantastic'	vogue word	DELETE
'fixtures or fittings'	legal pair	select one word and use it consistently

Expression	*Objection*	*Preferred options*
'for and during the period'	legal pair	select one word and use it consistently
'for the period of'	redundant words	DELETE or 'for'
'for the purpose of'	compound	'for'
'for the reason that'	compound	'because'
'forthwith'	archaic	DELETE or 'immediately'
'forward'	unfamiliar	'send'
'forward planning'	tautology	DELETE
'free and complete'	legal pair	select one word and use it consistently
'frightful'	vogue word	DELETE
'full and complete'	legal pair	select one word and use it consistently
'full and final'	legal pair	select one word and use it consistently
'further' (as in 'it is further agreed that' or 'it is subject to a further condition that')	redundant	can usually be deleted; it is usually unnecessary or indicates that there are two clauses of the same nature (e.g. conditions), which could be grouped together in one clause
'give, devise and bequeath'	legal triplet	select one word and use it consistently
'give notice'	unfamiliar	'notify'
'good and effectual'	legal pair	select one word and use it consistently
'good and sufficient'	legal pair	select one word and use it consistently
'goods and chattels'	legal pair	select 'goods' unless you wish to include money other than sterling or choses in action
'had and received'	legal pair	select one word and use it consistently

Expression	Objection	Preferred options
'hereafter'	archaic	DELETE or 'below' or 'in the future'
'hereby'	archaic	DELETE
'herein'	archaic	DELETE or 'in this Agreement'
'hereinafter'	archaic	DELETE or 'below'
'hereinafter referred to as'	archaic	DELETE – insert term defined in quotes in brackets: 'Anthony King (the "Borrower")'
'hereinbefore'	archaic	DELETE or 'above'
'hereof'	archaic	DELETE or 'of this Agreement'
'hereto'	archaic	DELETE or 'to this Agreement'
'hereunder'	archaic	DELETE or 'in this agreement'
'hereunto'	archaic	DELETE
'herewith'	archaic	in a letter: DELETE or 'we enclose' or 'enclosed is' 'attached is'; in agreements: 'with this Agreement'
'howsoever'	archaic	'in any way'
'if at any time' and 'from time to time'	unfamiliar	'whenever'
'important essentials'	tautology	select one word and use it consistently
'important to add'	redundant	DELETE
'in accordance with [the provisions/terms and conditions/of]'	compound	'under' or 'by'
'in advance of'	compound	'before'
'in all likelihood'	abstract	'probably'
'in connection with'	compound	'with', 'about' or concerning'
'in excess of'	compound	'exceeds'
'in favour of'	compound	'for'

Expression	Objection	Preferred options
'in order to'	compound	'to'
'in relation to'	compound	'about', 'with', or 'concerning'
'in some instances'	compound	'sometimes'
'in so far as'	redundant words	DELETE
'in terms of'	compound	DELETE or 'about', 'for'
'in the event that'	compound	'if'
'in the pipeline'	cliché	DELETE
'in toto'	foreign	'completely', 'as a whole'
'inasmuch as'	compound	'since'
'initiate'	unfamiliar	'start' or 'begin'
'inputs'	abstract	rephrase using more specific words
'inter alia'	foreign	'among other things'
'interaction'	vogue word/abstract	rephrase using more specific words
'interesting to point out'	redundant	DELETE
'interfacing'	vogue word	DELETE
'ipso facto'	foreign	DELETE or 'automatically' or 'by the fact itself'
'it should be noted'	redundant	DELETE
'last will and testament'	legal pair	select one word and use it consistently
'made and entered into'	legal pair	select one word and use it consistently
'majority of instances'	compound	'usually' or 'most'
'marginalise'	vogue word	DELETE
'market-place'	cliché	'market'
'materialise'	vogue word	DELETE
'means and includes'	redundant words	'means'
'meaningful'	vogue word	DELETE
'mutatis mutandis'	foreign	instead specify changes i.e. 'shall apply as if references to 'X' were to 'Y' or 'with the necessary changes'

Expression	*Objection*	*Preferred options*
'mutually agree'	tautology	DELETE 'mutually' (if they agree it must be mutual)
'naked truth'	cliché	DELETE
'nice'	vogue word	DELETE
'nominate, constitute and appoint'	redundant words	'appoint'
'null and void' and the tautologous 'totally null and void'	legal pair	select either 'null' or 'void'; DELETE 'totally'
'of the first part'	redundant/archaic	DELETE
'of the one part'	redundant/archaic	DELETE
'on a [weekly/regular] basis'	compound	'weekly', 'regularly'
'one iota'	cliché	DELETE
'operation'	abstract	rephrase using more specific words
'order and direct'	legal pair	select one word and use it consistently
'parameter'	over-used metaphor	avoid
'pari passu'	foreign	'equally'
'past history'	tautology	select one word and use it consistently
'per annum'	foreign	a year
'per your request'	clichéd antique formula	DELETE
'perform and discharge'	legal pair	select one word and use it consistently
'peruse'	unfamiliar	'read', 'study', 'examine', 'review' or 'consider'
'phenomenal'	vogue word	DELETE
'pillar to post'	cliché	DELETE
'please find [enclosed]' (in a letter)	clichéd formula	DELETE
'post hoc'	foreign	'after this'
'pretty'	vogue word	DELETE
'price tag'	cliché	'price'

Expression	Objection	Preferred options
'prima facie'	foreign	'sufficient evidence unless the contrary is proved'
'prior to'	unfamiliar	'before'
'pro tem'	foreign	'for the time being', 'temporarily'
'pro tanto'	foreign	'to the extent that' or 'to that extent'
'provided [always; that]'	archaic	'if' or 'but'
'pursuant to'	unfamiliar	'under'
'repair and make good'	legal pair	select one word and use it consistently
'rest, residue and remainder'	legal triplet	select one word and use it consistently
'save and except'	legal pair	select one word and use it consistently
'said' or even worse, 'aforesaid' or 'aforementioned'	archaic	DELETE or 'the', or if absolutely necessary 'that' or 'those'
'[to be] 'seised of'	archaic	[to] own
'sensational'	vogue word	DELETE
'settle and compromise'	legal pair	select one word and use it consistently
'shall have' in terms of setting out conditions (e.g. 'in the event the Borrower shall have failed')	unfamiliar	in most contexts 'if the Borrower fails'
'situation'	abstract	rephrase using more specific words
'so to do'	unfamiliar	'to do so'
'subsequent to'	unfamiliar	'after'
'such' when used in a similar way to 'said'	ambiguous	DELETE or 'the' or 'that' or 'those'
'suffer or permit'	legal pair	select one word and use it consistently

Expression	Objection	Preferred options
'super'	vogue word	DELETE
'syndrome'	vogue word/over-used metaphor	DELETE
'systematise'	vogue word	DELETE
'taken by storm'	cliché	DELETE
'talk turkey'	cliché	DELETE
'terms and conditions of' [the Agreement]	redundant	DELETE (references to an agreement can usually only mean its terms and conditions) or use 'terms of' or 'provisions of'
'terrible'	vogue word	DELETE
'terrific'	vogue word	DELETE
'that particular'	redundant/archaic	'that'
'that parties hereto hereby agree the one with the other'	archaic formula	DELETE or, if necessary, 'it is agreed'
'the parties hereto have hereunto set their hands and seals'	archaic formula	'executed by the parties as a deed'
'the same'	archaic	'it'; 'them'
'thereby'	archaic	'by it', 'by them', 'by [name of agreement]' or 'in that manner'
'therefor'	archaic	'for it', 'for them'
'therein'	archaic	DELETE or 'there' or 'in it' or 'in the [document/property]'
'thereof'	archaic	DELETE or 'of it'
'thereto'	archaic	'to it', 'to them'
'thereunder'	archaic	'under it' or 'under [name of agreement]'
'totally'; 'totally [e.g. unique; unanimous]'	over-used qualifying word; tautologous qualification of an absolute	DELETE
'track record'	cliché	'record'
'tremendous'	vogue word	DELETE

Expression	*Objection*	*Preferred options*
'tried and tested'	tautologous pair	select one word and use it consistently
'true and correct'	legal pair	select one word and use it consistently
'under separate cover'	clichéd antique formula	DELETE or 'separately'
'undertake and agree'	legal pair	select one word and use it consistently
'unholy alliance'	cliché	DELETE
'unless and until'	legal pair	select one word and use it consistently
'until such time as'	redundant words	'until'
'unto'	archaic	'to'
'utilise'	unfamiliar	'use'
'variables'	abstract	rephrase using more specific words
'very'; 'very [true; unanimous; unique]	over-used qualifying word/tautology qualification of an absolute	DELETE
vice versa	foreign	'conversely', 'the order being reversed'
'view with alarm'	cliché	DELETE
'well and sufficiently'	legal pair	select one word and use it consistently
'whatsoever'	archaic	DELETE; 'any' alone is usually sufficient or 'whatever'
'whereas'	archaic	DELETE
'whereby'	archaic	'under which' or 'by which'
'whereof'	archaic	DELETE or 'of which'
'wheresoever'	archaic	DELETE or 'wherever'
'whomsoever' or 'whosoever'	archaic	DELETE or 'who ever'
'with a view to'	compound	'to'
'with reference to'; 'with respect to'	compound	'on', 'about' or 'concerning'
'witnesseth'	archaic	'witnesses'

Expression	Objection	Preferred options
'wonderful'	vogue word	DELETE
'writing on the wall'	cliché	DELETE
'your esteemed favour'	clichéd formula	DELETE
'your good selves'	clichéd formula	DELETE or 'you' or [name or names of person or persons]

Bibliography

Adler, Mark, *Clarity for Lawyers* (London: Law Society, 1990).

Aitken, James K, *Piesse the Elements of Drafting*, 7th ed. (Australia: The Law Book Company Ltd, 1987).

Blake, Susan, *Legal Advice and Drafting*, 4th ed. (London: Blackstone Press Ltd, 1987).

Coode, George, On Legislative Expression, Report of the Poor Law Commissioners on Local Taxation, House of Commons Papers, 1843, Vol XX.

Cutts, Martin and Maher, *The Plain English Story* (The Plain English Campaign, 1988).

Cutts, Martin, *Unspeakable Acts* (Words at Work, 1993).

Ehrlich, Eugene, *Nil Desperandum* (Guild Publishing, 1986).

Fowler, Henry, *Modern English Usage*, 2nd ed. (Oxford: Oxford University Press, 1965).

Gowers, Ernest, *The Complete Plain Words*, 3rd ed. (HMSO, 1986).

McCrum, Robert et all, *The Story of English*, Revised edition (London: Faber and Faber, 1992).

National Consumer Council, *Plain Words for Lawyers* (1984).

Parker, Anthony, *Modern Conveyancing Precedents*, 2nd ed. (London: Butterworths, 1989).

Parker, Anthony, *Modern Wills Precedents*, 2nd ed. (London: Butterworths, 1987).

Partridge, Eric, *Usage and Abusage*, 6th ed. (London: Hamish Hamilton, 1965).

Phythian, Brian, *A Concise Dictionary of Correct English*, (Hodder and Stoughton Ltd, 1979).

Ramage, R. W., *Kelly's Draftsman*, 16th ed. (London: Butterworths, 1993).

Wydick, Richard, *Plain English for Lawyers*, 2nd ed. (Carolina Academic Press, 1985).